D1066166

Behind the Secret Window

A MEMOIR OF A HIDDEN CHILDHOOD
DURING WORLD WAR TWO

NELLY S. TOLL

PUFFIN BOOKS

Publisher's Note
This is a true story. All the events described in this book actually occurred,
but the identities of the people involved have been changed.

PUFFIN BOOKS
Published by the Penguin Group
Penguin Putnam Books for Young Readers,
345 Hudson Street, New York, New York 10014, U.S.A.
Penguin Books Ltd, 80 Strand, London WC2R ORL, England
Penguin Books Australia Ltd, 250 Camberwell Road, Camberwell, Victoria 3124, Australia
Penguin Books Canada Ltd, 10 Alcorn Avenue, Toronto, Ontario, Canada M4V 3B2
Penguin Books (N.Z.) Ltd, 182–190 Wairau Road, Auckland 10, New Zealand

Penguin Books Ltd, Registered Offices: Harmondsworth, Middlesex, England

First published in the United States of America by Dial Books,
a division of Penguin Books USA Inc., 1993
Published by Puffin Books,
a division of Penguin Putnam Books for Young Readers, 2003

1 3 5 7 9 10 8 6 4 2

THE LIBRARY OF CONGRESS HAS CATALOGED THE DIAL EDITION AS FOLLOWS:
Toll, Nelly S.
Behind the secret window : a memoir of a hidden childhood
during World War Two / by Nelly S. Toll.—1st ed.
p.   cm.
Summary: The author recalls her experiences when she and her mother were hidden from
the Nazis by a Gentile couple in Lwów, Poland, during World War II.
ISBN 0-8037-1362-2
1 Jews—Ukraine—L'vov—Persecutions—Juvenile literature. 2. Holocaust, Jewish
(1939–1945)—Ukraine—L'vov—Personal narratives—Juvenile literature.
3. Toll, Nelly S.—Juvenile literature.
4. World War, 1939–1945—children—Ukraine—L'vov—Juvenile literature.
5. L'vov (Ukraine)—Ethnic relations—Juvenile literature.
[1. Jews—Ukraine—L'vov—Persecutions.
2. Holocaust, Jewish (1939-1945)—Ukraine—L'vov—Personal narratives.
3. Toll, Nelly S. 4. World War, 1939–1945—Ukraine—L'vov.] I. Title.
DS135.R93L8976 1993
940.53'18'0947718—dc20 92-21831 CIP AC

Puffin Books ISBN 0-14-230241-4

Printed in the United States of America

This book is dedicated to the memory of

MY MOTHER
*a true heroine, who protected me from danger,
sheltered me from fear, eased my pain,
nurtured me with hope and loving tenderness,
and is the reason why I am here to tell this tale;*

MY COURAGEOUS FATHER
*who never hesitated to risk his life
in order to save ours;*

and

MY BELOVED LITTLE BROTHER, JANEK
whom I will never forget.

*This book is also consecrated to all the
innocent victims who perished in the Holocaust,
whose memory must never fade.*

Acknowledgments

I offer my deepest thanks to my husband for his love, concern, continuous dedication, and total support as I wrote this book.

I also wish to thank my children, Sharon and Jeffrey, whose names immortalize the memory of my father and brother, for their loving affection and belief in the worth of my work; and my son-in-law, Barry, and daughter-in-law, Gail, for their caring and encouragement.

My appreciation goes to my sister, Bettina, who together with Henek made our family whole again, and to her husband and children for their good wishes; to my extended family for their interest; to all my friends who expressed their support for the importance of my written and visual material, including my former art and art history professor, Dr. Burton Wasserman, for his absolute faith in my watercolors; to Nagle Jackson, Artistic Director of the McCarter Theater in Princeton, New Jersey, who years ago thought my diary significant enough to put it on stage; to Claire Berger for her editorial assistance and interest in my writing twenty years ago; to my former professor of history, Sid Kessler, for his confidence in my work and for his knowledge; to Renia, for caring about every step of my book and for sharing my joy; and to Dr. Robert Blumberg, for long ago believing in the value of my art and writing and for his continuous friendship.

| Acknowledgments |

I must also express my thanks here to all the interested individuals, institutions, and museums who exhibited my art and who continue to do so, including the Yad Vashem Museum in Israel.

In particular, I thank William Rubel of the Children's Art Foundation in Santa Cruz, California, for his friendship, his unabated belief in the necessity of this book, his unflagging dedication to my art, and his desire to share my watercolor pictures with a large audience, which resulted in the first comprehensive exhibition of my work at the Judah Magnes Museum in Berkeley and the University of California at Santa Cruz.

Many thanks to my friend Dr. Yehuda Nir for his understanding, continuous interest, and fundamental belief in the importance of this book.

I gratefully acknowledge the help of Dr. Hayim Y. Sheynin, archivist and librarian of Gratz College, Philadelphia, for his expert reading of the manuscript for historical accuracy, and to Dr. David S. Wyman for his scholarly advice.

Finally, I owe much gratitude to my very special editor, Cindy Kane, for her commitment and sensitivity to this work, which found a safe home with Dial Books after many years. Her keen editorial discernment, her delicacy, sympathy, consideration, and friendship will not be forgotten.

Preface

As a child in poland during the Second World War, I began to keep *notatki*, notes, from the day the Germans entered Lwów, my birthplace, in 1941. Two years later, when my mother and I were hidden from the Nazis by a Christian couple who risked their lives to save ours, I began to develop those notes into a diary in which I described what I had seen and experienced from the year 1941.

This small black diary was very important to me. Using the logic of a child, I invented my own code that I called my "Esperanto," my universal language, and converted such dangerous words as "ghetto" and "Jews" into it. I reasoned that, if the Gestapo ever found my writing, they would not realize that I was Jewish and thus would not destroy it! In the foreword of my diary I wrote, "If I should be killed, at least my *pamiętnik* (memory book) will stay alive so that the whole world can see the terrible things that happened to us."

This journal was my place for recording the frightening reality of my existence during those dark days—unlike the paintings that I created at the same time, which provided me with an escape into a fantasy world. I painted over sixty watercolors, made up cheerful tales about them, and sewed the pictures and stories together into small booklets with white thread; through the magic of art, I became a part of that happy world of illusion.

The five-by-seven-inch and seven-by-ten-inch sheets of paper were filled with colorful flowers, blue skies, loving adults, and carefree children busy with normal daily activities. Only symbolically did they reflect my feelings of apprehension about the constant danger surrounding us.

Through captions, I have tried to suggest the origins of the paintings reproduced in this book. My influences ranged from stories obtained from the library by the same courageous neighbor who bought my paper and paints, to memories of my father and little brother, to fragments of my life before the war, to my wish for a friend my own age. These pictures do not directly illustrate my story, but they are very much a part of it.

My "brush trips" always led me back to my little black journal—the only private part of my life in our tiny room. The diary is the basis for this memoir, and if there are gaps of time that are not as fully explained as others here, it is because my experiences from those times were not as clearly imprinted in my mind.

I never discussed my writing with my mother; it was too private. I felt differently about my gentle pictures, which I shared with her. It was her support that helped me pass those long, isolated, and frightening days, taught me how to see the world in brighter hues, and turned my sadness into hope.

To this day, I have not shown my little diary to her, although I keep her well informed about its journey—and that of my paintings—into a better world.

Nelly S. Toll, June 1992

Historical Note

AFTER GERMANY was defeated in World War I, the country experienced economic depression and political crisis. Against this background, an extreme right-wing political party called the National Socialist (Nazi) movement flourished, and a previously unknown war veteran named Adolf Hitler quickly rose to power. After Hitler became chancellor of Germany in 1933, he developed the country's military industry, providing employment for many working-class people who became loyal supporters of the Nazi party and of their *"Führer"* (leader).

From the beginning, Hitler used written and visual Nazi propaganda to blame Jewish people and Communists for all of Germany's ills. He stressed the need to make the country free of all the Jews and other "undesirables" in order to return it to prosperity, and he impressed upon his countrymen the notion that Germany was only for the Aryans—white Christians of a well-defined ethnic background.

Hitler's long-range ambition was to conquer new land for Germany throughout Europe. In 1938 he expanded his control into Austria and Czechoslovakia; not until his army invaded

Poland in 1939 did Britain, France, and Canada declare war on Germany. Winston Churchill, the British prime minister, pledged to support the Soviet Union when it was invaded by Germany in 1941; America entered the war in December of that year, after the bombing of Pearl Harbor by Japan. These "Allied" nations were pitted against Germany and the other "Axis" countries, Italy and Japan, that joined its fight.

When Hitler came to power, he, his administration, and the German legislature issued orders and set up laws authorizing the persecution of Jews through acts of terrorism and economic deprivation. As the war escalated, he moved to his ultimate priority: the complete destruction of Europe's eleven million Jews. A special meeting, the Wannsee Conference, was held in January 1942 to coordinate the details of this "Final Solution of the Jewish Question" (as the mass murders were called) among various government departments.

An important part of the "Final Solution" was the development of two kinds of camps for the Jewish people and undesirable Gentiles: labor camps such as Lwów's Janowska camp, Buchenwald, and many others, where thousands of victims died of starvation, torture, and exhaustion; and the highly secret extermination camps, which were equipped with gas chambers designed for the killing of Jews.

Hitler put his plan into effect with extraordinary precision, meeting with no opposition from world leaders. The mass killings took place with speed and brutal force in such infamous death camps as Auschwitz-Birkenau, Treblinka, Majdanek, Chełmno, Bełżec, and others.

As early as November 1942, the United States administration, including the State Department and President Roosevelt, knew about the mass murder of Europe's Jews and yet did nothing to rescue them throughout the following fourteen months. Only after that long delay was limited action taken through the War Refugee Board. Information about the inhumane operations at Auschwitz was known to the American government well before the end of the war, yet the pleas of Jewish leaders to bomb the railroads leading to the extermination camp were dismissed—despite the fact that American bomber planes struck German factories near the Auschwitz gas chambers on several occasions in 1944.

Only one country—small, neutral Denmark—stands out in its active opposition to the German attempt to massacre its Jewish citizens. Invaded by Germany in 1940, the Danes resisted German rule until their liberation, and they managed to smuggle a large part of their Jewish population to safety in Sweden.

Germany was defeated by the American, British, and Russian Allies in 1945. When the war ended, six million Jews had died; over one million of these were children.

Part One

Lwów, Poland · June 1941 to Spring 1943

1

I WILL NEVER FORGET watching from a balcony on a warm, sunny day in June 1941 as the German army marched through the streets of Lwów. I was at my aunt's apartment with my little brother, Janek, and our three cousins. Karol, Ninka, Janek, and I were pushing each other to get a better look at the crowded street below. Only Sewer, my oldest cousin, seemed above it all; he stood quietly looking over our shoulders.

Skarbkowska Street was filled with adults and children throwing flowers at the German soldiers. Loud music, laughter, and congratulatory shouts all mixed with the sound of marching boots. The Germans were heroes; they had defeated the Russians, who had occupied our city for nearly two years and were hated by many Ukrainian and Polish people.

A red balloon flew past our balcony and floated into the sky to join hundreds of yellow, red, and blue ones. It was like a great parade. I wanted to be there celebrating with the others, but we children were not allowed to go downstairs. Aunt Elsa and Mama had gone down to see the crowd after telling Sewer to watch us.

My aunt did not explain why we had to stay in the apartment. She was strict—not at all like my mama. But since we all lived with Aunt Elsa now, we had no choice but to listen to her.

I looked for Papa in the crowd. He had gone into hiding right after the Soviet army invaded Lwów in October 1939, and I hadn't seen him since. He'd had to leave quickly; the Russians considered him a "bourgeois"—a property holder—and therefore an undesirable member of society. My family was afraid they would send him away to a labor camp in Siberia.

His disappearance had been a big secret. When I asked Mama where he was going she would only say, "On a long journey to safety." It was better for me not to know, I found out later, in case I was questioned. But now that the Russians were gone, Mama assured me that he would be returning soon.

"Everything will be like it was before the Russians came," Sewer told me as we watched the crowd.

"Everything?" I asked. Secretly I hoped that our maid, Magda, and our governess, Dana—both of whom I missed very much—would come back to live with us too, once we returned to our apartment on Plac Smolki (Smolki Square).

"Yes," Sewer responded. "The Germans are civilized people—educated and intelligent. Everyone, including Grandpa Henryk, thinks so."

That made sense. Grandpa Henryk was smart, a chess player. But for some reason I was annoyed with

Sewer's assurance. Sometimes he acted as if he was some kind of walking encyclopedia, and I got mad at him. After all, he was only fourteen years old—he didn't have to pretend that he was Uncle Leon himself!

It was true that Aunt Elsa had instructed us to listen to him because he was the oldest. Karol, who was ten, was next; then me, age six; then Janek, who was four, and then adorable, huggable little Ninka, whose fourth birthday we had just celebrated. With her curly blond hair and blue eyes, Ninka looked just like Sewer. Even though he could sound like a know-it-all, we all liked him; none of us could stay mad at him for long.

Suddenly, in the middle of all the happy commotion from the street, there was a loud shout: "Goddamn Jew!" Karol almost lost his black-rimmed glasses as he leaned over the railing and pointed to the corner, where a couple of German soldiers were beating up an old man with their rifles. As he fell down on the sidewalk, a crowd gathered around and started to laugh. To my horror, a few people even clapped their hands.

Then the door was yanked open, and Mama and Aunt Elsa were running toward the balcony. "Get inside immediately!" Aunt Elsa ordered, while Mama grabbed Janek's and Ninka's hands and pulled them into the apartment.

"But why were the soldiers beating up the man?" Janek asked Mama. "What did he do?"

"I don't know," Mama replied sharply. She told us we were not to talk about it and should forget what we had seen. We were not to return to the terrace under any circumstances, she warned us.

"I wish we could go back to our own apartment," I

3

confided to Sewer after Mama and Aunt Elsa had gone into the kitchen, whispering to each other. Then Janek started to cry, and Mama came out and took him back into the kitchen with her.

The rest of us went into the room I shared with Ninka. Karol's arms were wrapped around my little cousin, who was holding her porcelain doll tightly.

"Why didn't anyone stop the soldiers?" I asked Sewer, who shook his head and looked seriously troubled. This time he did not have an answer. The room was suddenly very quiet except for the buzzing of a fly. We were all frightened.

If only Papa would come back! I thought. He knew everything, and he always had answers.

2

My LIFE BEFORE THE RUSSIANS came was very happy. I was still too young to go to school; my days had revolved around Mama, Papa, and Janek, my cousins and small friends, and visits to my grandparents and to Papa's store.

I could remember building castles out of sugar cubes on the wooden counter of Papa and Grandpa Josef's wholesale dry-goods store. Papa would let me help myself to barley, rice, and beans from the big burlap bags that stood in the corner, and I would pile them on top of my palace until it collapsed under the weight. When I cried from disappointment, Papa would scoop me up in his arms and kiss the tears away.

I was very close to all my grandparents and would visit them often. My father's parents, *Babcia* (Grandma) Tyncia and Grandpa Josef, lived below us in our apartment building on Plac Smolki, one of several buildings owned by Papa. At every opportunity I would run downstairs to see my *babcia*, whose velvety black eyes would light up in her wrinkled face when she saw me coming through the back entrance.

My grandma was short and full-figured, with thin lips and a square jaw. Although I loved her, many people—including Mama—did not like her. A few times I had overheard Zosia, their maid, gossiping with Kasia, our live-in seamstress, about *Babcia* and Aunt Regina, my father's sister. My aunt was considered to be somewhat eccentric, and my grandmother was strict and demanding with her servants. Some people called her a "Xantippa" for the bad-tempered wife of Socrates.

But to me, *Babcia* Tyncia was wonderful. She would often give me presents for no special reason—"Just because I love you," she would say. My favorite gift was a small ruby ring that she had put on my pinky finger just before Rosh Hashanah, telling me never to take it off. I kept it on even during my bath.

On Thursdays we would count all her shiny coins, *groszy* (pennies), then put them into my small black purse. I saved them for my favorite red-bearded beggar, who had no arms or legs and sat in a little cart near the cinema across the street. Every Friday I would bring him all my *groszy*, and he would smile, showing me his only two teeth.

Friday was a special day at Grandma Tyncia's; together with her maid, she would prepare a big Sabbath meal. Sometimes I watched them, or else I went to see the fish floating and jumping in my grandma's bathtub before it was killed for dinner. Once I saw the cook chop its head off on a wooden board, but I never wanted to watch it again after that time; it was too bloody.

Saturday was supposed to be a day of rest. Our store was closed, and Grandpa went to pray in the synagogue. But to me, it meant visits with the family, with lots of eating and good times together.

In the long winter afternoons, I would sit on my grandma's windowsill, her arms wrapped around me, and listen to her colorful stories about the past. I would stay till dusk, watching the snowflakes fall on the black *dorożki* (horse-drawn carriages) galloping on the street below.

Babcia Tyncia's hands moved all the time as she talked, and her dark eyes (which she said I'd inherited from her) would shine with excitement. She would tell me that I was the prettiest little girl in the city of Lwów and that when I grew up, I would have all the boys running after me. I would laugh, and she would too.

Sometimes, from the corner of my eyes, I would watch *Ciocia* (Aunt) Regina silently moving around from room to room, careful on the slippery lacquered parquet floor in her fashionable high-heeled shoes. I thought she was pretty. Tall, with dark eyes and pitch-black hair, she resembled Papa, but unlike him she rarely smiled. I don't remember *Ciocia* Regina ever doing anything except spending a lot of time and concentration on rolling her hair on shiny brown rollers, until her whole head was covered with rows and rows of curlers that sharply outlined her white powdered face.

She spent almost every day at home—or at least, I

never saw her leave the apartment or have any guests, with the exception of "Uncle" Zygo, a distant relative who came weekly to visit her. Although Mama told me that this Zygo had become Aunt Regina's husband, the servants thought otherwise. They said that it was not a true marriage, only a pretext, since my aunt Regina continued to live with my grandparents.

Of course I did not understand any of this, and no one was going to explain it to me either. It was not for children, I was often told, so I had to listen to gossips like Zosia. In between washing clothes on her washboard or cooking them in big, steaming vats that made the kitchen foggy, she would explain to Kasia the reason for my grandma's frequent anger. "She takes all the bad luck she has with *Pani* (Mrs.) Regina," Zosia would say, "and pours it all on our weary heads. Some day she will pay for it, the tyrant! Everybody has his time!"

Zosia was long gone now, the same as our servants who'd had to leave when the Russians came. Rosy-cheeked Magda and tall, pretty Dana had to move out almost immediately. Domestic help was not allowed under the Soviet regime; it was against the Communist doctrine. But more dreadful than all the other losses had been Papa's disappearance.

I remembered how I'd had to hold back the tears swimming in my eyes while Papa kissed and hugged me good-bye in the narrow corridor of our apartment house. The building no longer belonged to us, since ownership of private property was forbidden by the Soviet government.

About two days after Papa vanished into the night,

a handsome Russian major with shiny brown boots and an entourage of loud-voiced soldiers moved into our apartment.

Major Davidovich was a devoted Communist whose chest was decorated with many medals. He allowed us to stay in one of our four bedrooms, even though he didn't have to do it. He was very friendly to all of us, speaking French to Mama, asking her to help him shop for his family back in Moscow, and showering Janek and me with big pieces of bittersweet chocolate and even imported oranges. These were luxury items, not easily available.

I liked Major Davidovich, and even though I did not understand Russian, I sensed in his broad smile and the twinkle in his watery blue eyes that he meant well and liked us too. He called Mama "Comrade Landau," took her to special stores, and tried to help her with all the responsibilities that now rested on her shoulders.

Even people changed after the Russians came. Władek, our friendly janitor, and his toothless, chubby wife—who before used to bring Janek and me hot, puffy doughnuts covered with powdered sugar—now would not even look at me when I said hello.

Because he now claimed to be a staunch Communist, Władek was allowed to move, free of charge, to a bigger apartment on the sixth floor, just above ours. And when Major Davidovich was called back to Moscow months later, Władek helped the major's soldiers carry our furniture out.

I remember how sad I was as I watched them packing our piano, crystals, figurines, and paintings into big wooden crates filled with straw. When I saw them taking Papa's favorite picture, I asked, in the broken Russian I had learned, "Why are you taking *all* our things?"

"They are needed more in Moscow," a young soldier explained.

I wondered if the hand-painted headboard of my bed and blue armoire would now be used by some strange Russian girl. The only thing the soldiers could not take were the beautiful porcelain stoves, decorated with ornate animals and geometric designs, which were rooted like trees from the floor to the high ceilings of each room.

When Major Davidovich came into the living room and saw how unhappy I looked, he gave me a big piece of chocolate, picked me up, and started to dance around the room, trying to make me laugh. Then he performed a quick Russian *kozaczka* dance, squatting low to the floor, just as his soldiers did on the late nights when Janek and I secretly spied on their parties from behind the French doors of our salon. They would drink Mama's perfume, since they couldn't get any vodka, and their girlfriends would wear her nightgowns, thinking they were evening dresses!

Mama did not find out about those secret evenings until much later, after Major Davidovich was replaced. His successor was Officer Volodarov, who brought a big truckload of furniture with him and was very polite and reserved. He also spoke French to Mama. But we remained in the apartment only until his beautiful wife arrived. Then we had to leave and move to Aunt Elsa's, where Janek told Mama all about how we had watched the soldiers.

I was happy when we moved to my aunt's apartment. At least now I could be with my cousins; we always had fun together. But almost immediately Mama was told by the Soviet authorities that she had to get a job in order to live productively like all other Communist citizens, so she began to work in a dairy store.

Aunt Elsa, Mama's sister, was going to take care of us kids until her visa from my uncle in Australia arrived. Her husband, Uncle Leon—whom all of us liked very much—left Poland just before the war broke out to find a better life for his family. They were going to join him in Melbourne, once he landed a suitable position and an apartment.

We hadn't heard anything at all from my uncle since the Germans came. My aunt was hoping for some news from him—a note or maybe even a letter about the visa—but she had no luck. Only Grandpa Henryk believed that good news would arrive shortly; he always looked on the bright side.

I knew I would miss Aunt Elsa and my cousins if they ever left for Australia, but having Mama home with us again made the thought more bearable. Now that the Russians had been sent fleeing back to Moscow, she no longer had to work in the *Ruski* dairy store.

Best of all, now that the Soviet army was gone, Papa could leave his hiding place and come back to us. I'd had to pretend not to eavesdrop on Mama's conversations with Aunt Elsa about the secret little notes she received from Papa in his hideout near the Romanian border. When I asked her for the hundredth time when he was coming home, now that the danger was over, Mama told me once again that it wouldn't be too much longer.

"Just a few days," she said. Sewer agreed with Mama that Papa would be back soon, and I believed him because Sewer was usually right.

3

I THOUGHT A LOT ABOUT PAPA, especially at night when the stars came out or the sky, cold and black, engulfed our room in darkness. I tried to summon his presence by piecing together patches of make-believe conversation and recalling my fun times with him; then I would play with his fleeting image, never wanting to let him go.

I fantasized about Papa's return so often that when he finally came back one night in July, I almost could not believe it. When he planted a big kiss on my cheek, I opened my eyes and gave a shriek, then threw my arms around his neck and squeezed him with all my might. He lifted me, kissed me, and held me close. I could taste tears rolling down my face and was glad that neither Mama, who stood next to my bed, nor Papa could see them.

He spoke in a hushed voice, but he woke up little Ninka anyway. By the time he had rushed to the adjoining room to see Janek, all my cousins were up, and everyone was kissing and hugging Papa. For some reason—I did not understand why—the adults decided not to turn on the lights. We all sat down in the darkness of our living room; Janek and I each perched on one of Papa's knees.

Between hugs and kisses, questions and celebration, we stayed there until the morning sun started to break through the clouds. Then, suddenly, I grew scared.

"You're going to stay with us, aren't you, Papa?" I asked. "You're not going away again?"

"No, no, I won't," he assured me, then kissed us both again and led us back to our beds. I remember thinking that now that Papa had returned, everything really would be the way it was before.

But it was not. We did not go back to our own apartment. "Not yet," Papa said when I asked him. "We have to stay with Aunt Elsa for a while longer, and then we will see."

Though he was suddenly vague about our return to Plac Smolki, he did explain about some other things. Grandma Tyncia and Grandpa Josef were ill, he told me, and they needed someone to take care of them. This was his responsibility, he said, and he wanted me to understand that he would be spending some time with his parents; sometimes he might even have to stay overnight with them.

"I'm the only one they have to count on, since all the servants are gone," he said. "But I will always come back," he added as he saw me struggling with tears. He held me in his arms and covered my cheeks with little kisses.

14

It didn't make sense to me. *Babcia* Tyncia, Grandpa Josef, and Aunt Regina still lived in the apartment building on Plac Smolki. If we returned, Papa would not have to spend so much time away—he would just walk down two floors to see his family. But Skarbkowska Street was far away—and besides, how could Papa take care of them and get a job? I'd heard him whisper to Mama that it was very important for him to find one—that it was "the safest thing to do."

What did this mean? When I asked Sewer, he explained that my parents had meant it was "safest" to work for the Germans since they were in power now.

"Things do not look so good for Jewish people these days," he said. He told me about the anti-Jewish placards that he had seen on some of the street buildings, and the decree that had been posted all around the city ordering all Jews over fourteen years of age to wear yellow armbands with Jewish stars. Anyone who did not follow these orders would be severely punished.

"But I won't wear one," Sewer announced. He said that he could pass for a Gentile with his blond hair. No matter how much Aunt Elsa tried to reason with him, he walked around town without an armband.

Not long after Papa's return, both he and Mama found jobs working in a factory that manufactured clothing for the German army. I was glad, because this seemed to be very safe. Sewer began looking for a job too. Strange stories were circulating, he said; he would not tell me any more, but I knew the rumors were bad because my parents began whispering together and looking scared.

Mama and Aunt Elsa had forbidden us kids—except for Sewer—to go out on the street. No one wanted to hear about how much I missed my grandparents. On the last day of July, I decided to ignore my mother's rule and go to visit Grandma Fancia and Grandpa Henryk, whom I had not seen for a while. It was a warm day, and I was feeling bored and sad.

I was able to sneak out when Aunt Elsa and Sewer were not looking, and as I turned the corner of Skarbkowska Street I waved to Anka, Tadek, and Adamek— neighboring children with whom I sometimes played. But as I continued on my way, I suddenly felt a sharp pain near my neck. I turned quickly and looked behind me, and to my horror saw little stones flying toward me.

"Jew, dirty Jew! Go back to Palestine! Go, dirty Jew!" shouted the three children. I started to run back to the apartment as fast as I could, hearing their feet and laughter behind me.

Moments later I flew into our building and ran up the three flights of steps to find Sewer in the corridor, just closing the door. I fell into his arms and started to cry.

"Why are they throwing stones at me? Why?" I repeated. I wished that Mama were there, but I knew that she was working and would not come home until late.

Sewer tried to calm me, wiping my tears. We sat down on the steps, and with his arms around me I felt safe again. "Anti–Semitism, hatred of the Jews, is getting worse," he explained, "although you should know that we have been scapegoats for hundreds of years. You don't remember, but just before the war, a

16

group of university students broke the window of Grandma Fancia's fabric store, and even after they vandalized everything, the police didn't do anything."

"But those kids were our friends before the Germans came," I said. "Why would they suddenly hate me and call me names now? I didn't do anything wrong!"

"Grandpa Henryk says this hatred is like a poisonous snake," Sewer told me. "It will probably move on in time. A few hundred Jews might get killed; then it will be quiet again."

I asked Sewer what we should do about this hate for now. He said that we should all try to leave Poland as soon as possible.

"But how will we get visas?" I asked. "Can your father send them for us too?"

Sewer answered that Papa should try to get the exit visas somehow. "Your papa has connections," he told me. I did not understand what he meant by "connections," but I didn't want him to know it, so I said nothing. I only wished that we could all leave together; I wanted to talk about this to Papa.

That evening Mama came home bruised black and blue all over, with a swollen eye. At first she told us that she had fallen, but then the terrible truth came out.

She had been beaten up by a Ukrainian policeman when she accidentally dropped an egg at the market. The policeman ordered her to get on her knees and scrub the sidewalk. Then he hit her, slapped her face, and cursed her while everybody on the street watched. Mama pretended to act cheerful to us kids, but I knew that she was scared.

I could not tell her what had happened to me; I

17

didn't want to make her even more unhappy. She told us that her eye really did not hurt her; it was just a bad bruise. But then she stressed again, in a very strict voice, that we were never, *never* to go on the street. Sewer was the only one who could.

4

CHANGES WERE HAPPENING FAST in Lwów. New German rules were continuously appearing: Jewish children were forbidden to attend school, Aryans were no longer allowed to work for Jews, and a curfew had been posted. Our frowning parents would often send us to our rooms while they discussed the rules in hushed voices. We were still living with Aunt Elsa, and I now knew that our apartment on Plac Smolki had been taken over by the Germans.

Aunt Elsa's living room became a gathering place for friends and neighbors eager to hear details about the progress of my aunt's Australian visa and to talk about other ways to escape the German madness. We could hear them in our room as we played American cowboys and Indians, so well described in the books of our favorite author, Karl May. They argued on and on about whether it was better to try to escape or to try to get "Christian papers," and how to get visas for

Australia, Cuba, South America, or Africa—if it was not too late already.

The names of my parents' friends, the Hertz family, were brought up in the conversation one evening. They had left for America secretly—in the middle of the night—just before the war broke out. There was much nervous speculation about their motives. Someone said that they probably *had* to run because of some trouble with the Polish law. "Otherwise," said this voice, "why should *anybody in his right mind* want to leave his business and properties and *escape* without even saying good-bye to anyone? *Only* criminals and *gangsters* scared of being thrown in jail emigrate to America. Everyone knows that! What do you think, it is so good out there? Does New York's gold pour from heaven, like some manna?"

"No, no, there's no need to panic," declared *Pan* Doctor Gross. (*Pan*, *Pani*, and *Panna* were respectful words—almost like saying "Sir," "Madam," or "Miss"— usually reserved for educated, well-spoken, so-called "better people.") "Because of a few anti–Semitic incidents by some fanatic Jew haters," the Doctor went on, "our people are getting hysterical."

"Is that so?" Mama asked.

"My dear *Pani,* don't believe him," said *Pani* Halina. "Danger is here to stay. We'd all better do something quickly!"

At this point, Karol suggested we open our door a bit. Now we could see as well as hear. Nobody noticed.

"What about all the stories about *Kristallnacht*?" someone asked. (We kids did not know what this

20

meant. Sewer later told me it was a night of terror all over Germany, three years before, when thousands of Jewish businesses were destroyed and many innocent Jews were killed and tortured.)

"Don't believe them!" *Pan* Nachów said, thoughtfully stroking his gray beard as he looked around at the others. "All that nasty gossip was probably invented by some young Communists to stir up anger."

Mama told him that Grandpa Henryk, whose whole family lived in Vienna and were better informed about the German threat than we were, was very frightened.

Still, this *Pan* did not believe there was reason to be afraid. "The Germans are too civilized; it will pass," he insisted. Others looked unsure. Maybe he was right?

"Be patient, ignore it, don't worry so much" were *Pan* Nachów's last words as the door closed behind him. He was shot down the next day, as he was leaving the marketplace after exchanging *złoty* for produce. I was terribly scared when I heard about this. What was going to happen to us? Would they shoot us too?

Sewer, still only fourteen, went to work at the factory with Mama and Papa. We younger kids stayed indoors all the time now. No longer did I think of playing outside, feeling the summer's light breath, running in the rain, watching the reflections of shimmering puddles on our street. The adults looked worried and apprehensive, searching intently for answers. What to do next? Where to hide? When? Their questioning eyes were unsure, reflecting their fear, which we kids absorbed.

Magda, our superstitious former maid, had told me,

just before she left, that evil could come out of even the nicest men—that Lucifer could mysteriously poison them and turn them into someone else. I wondered if Hitler was a Lucifer, who had poisoned the Germans in this way.

I thought of Magda on the fearful afternoon when the German and Ukrainian police stormed into our building and banged on our neighbor's door. The population of Lwów had consisted of both Poles and Ukrainians; many of the Ukrainians became policemen to help the Gestapo, the secret police, persecute the Jews. I had been playing with my girlfriend, who lived on the floor below Aunt Elsa's, and had been just ready to enter our apartment when I saw the police in the corridor.

I quickly moved back and hid in the dark corner of the hallway. To my surprise, I heard unusually loud laughter from our neighbors, *Pani* Marzowa and *Panna* Jadzia, who were waving and calling out to the policemen. I decided to make a run for our apartment, but *Pani* Marzowa noticed me. Changing her pleasant voice to a mean one as suddenly as hail from a sunny sky, she yelled after me, "You deserve it, with all your money and jewelry, you *PARSZYWE ŻYDŁAKI!* (Dirty Jews!) Serves you right!"

I fell into our living room, still trembling, not understanding. Why did *Pani* Marzowa—the friendly and refined wife of a gymnasium (secondary school) professor—suddenly hate me? I hadn't done anything to her. I was always polite whenever we met in the hall. Was Grandma Tyncia right—even though Mama called it nonsense—when she said that anti–Semitism came with mother's milk?

I knew that even when Grandma was a little girl, she had hid in an underground hole while a wild mob of Polish and Ukrainian peasants raged wildly overhead, ready to kill every Jew in her village. She was lucky she was not murdered, like her father, a religious man with a long beard which they put on fire before they tortured and then killed him.

It was dangerous for Jews to have beards now also. Sewer told me the Germans did all kinds of mean things to observing Jews, but he would not tell me what. If we still had a telephone, like we did before the war, I would have called my grandpa Josef to tell him to shave off his goatee.

Then there came new German orders—to move all the Jews to a small section of town, forming a ghetto like the one that already existed in Warsaw. Gold and other valuables were to be delivered to the authorities. Respected Jewish community leaders were summoned by the Germans to expedite the assignments; their families too had to comply with these orders. We waited for our turn to come.

It did not matter that the large Jewish population of Lwów—approximately 150,000 people, nearly half of the city's inhabitants—was going to be squeezed together like sardines in a box. The Jews were no longer allowed to contaminate the Catholic part of town. I had thought that Polish Jews and Polish Catholics were the only religions that existed in the world; I now discovered as well that it was safer to be Catholic than Jewish.

Our order to move came on a windy day, around one o'clock in the afternoon. We were told that we had to be ready to leave in the next three hours! Even after Aunt Elsa gave the police her "safe working papers," which showed that she kept house for three family members who were employed in the German factory, it made no difference. "Three hours!" repeated the Ukrainian policeman. He was angry.

The German policeman spoke fast, and even though I did not understand what he said, I could see by the way he looked at us and then slammed the door that he too was mad. And then they were gone. Ninka started to cry. I ran to Janek, who was standing behind the doorway of his bedroom, sobbing. He grabbed my hand and wouldn't let go.

Aunt Elsa pressed her lips tightly and ran to the closet to get the suitcases out. We followed, and together we began to empty the dresser drawers and closets as fast as we could, throwing our things into valises and trunks. Aunt Elsa kept looking at her watch as we kids pushed clothes into the suitcases. Socks, underwear, pants, sweaters, coats, and dresses were strewn everywhere.

Even little Ninka was running around the room gathering different things, helping everyone. Aunt Elsa tried to talk to us calmly and tell us which closet or chest to empty next. But it was getting close to four o'clock, and there were still many things left in the closets and cabinets.

Ninka started to cry because no one had packed her toys. Aunt Elsa told her to stop, but Ninka would not. She grabbed her porcelain doll, Janina. We kids did not pay any attention to her as we ran from the living room to the bedroom.

Our time was almost up. We pulled on our wool coats and helped Karol to gather our luggage and put it near the door. We had to hurry.

Suddenly I saw Groźniak, the janitor, who never looked anybody in the eyes when he spoke, and his wife standing in our kitchen. They said they had come to help us with our packing.

"Do you think there is any way we could have more time?" Aunt Elsa asked.

Groźniak replied that he did not know how we could—"and truthfully," he added, "I do not want to be bothered with Jews and their problems." His wife just kept grinning. Then they both went to the bedroom and became very busy looking through all our closets.

A few minutes later I saw her quickly put some things in her apron pocket and then walk toward the front door holding some silver trays in her hand. I ran to Aunt Elsa, who was still in the bedroom, and whispered to her, but she told me to be quiet. "It does not matter," she said. Then Groźniak and his wife walked out without saying another word to us.

When our time was up, we all tried to carry our huge suitcases down the narrow steps to the backyard. I had never realized how strong Karol was. He had become a big help to Aunt Elsa, taking Sewer's place at home, even though no one had really told him that he should. He just kind of knew it.

Once downstairs we pushed and lifted our belongings to the cobblestoned backyard, where the other Jewish families with their children were gathering with their suitcases and boxes. There was no furniture.

Janek, Ninka, and I sat down on our trunks. We were told to stay there while Aunt Elsa and Karol walked over to some of the women whom we knew. There were no men. They were all working. A few of the families and their children were our friends, but no one else was leaving their spot in the yard. I overheard snatches of conversation filled with fear.

Then they came: the Ukrainian and German police. I watched them checking the belongings of other families in the left corner of the courtyard, and then a red-faced German with shiny boots walked straight up to us. Without even glancing at us he began to throw our clothes out of the suitcases. He was joined by the other policemen, who continued to rummage through our possessions, joking and laughing, until they reached the bottom. I don't remember all the things they took, only the gold watch that belonged to Grandpa Henryk, the binoculars, and Papa's camera. Aunt Elsa kept looking at their hands as they pulled our clothes out and threw them down on the ground, sometimes kicking them with their boots.

I did not move. Janek held my hand tight. We stood next to my aunt, who kept whispering to Ninka to stop crying. I felt the tears filling my eyes but would not allow them to spill out. The Ukrainian policeman gave Ninka a very angry look, spat on the ground, cursed, and then turned around and walked over to the next group.

I wished that Mama were with us, but I knew that she would be going from the factory to visit Grandma Fancia, who was sick, and would not be back until the evening. I wondered how she would find us. How would she and Papa know where we had moved to?

After the policemen left, Aunt Elsa told me that she would send Karol to the factory to let them know what had happened, and that I need not worry. Mama and Papa would find us; they would be with us tonight, she promised.

I don't remember how we finally got our belongings to the little house on Kleparowska Street. It was in the designated ghetto area, away from the Gentiles.

Our new house was smaller than our Skarbkowska Street apartment. We were very crowded. But that night when Mama and Papa came home and found us, I was so happy to be with them again that I did not care where we were. We were all together. Janek and I snuggled up with them in their bed, holding them, not letting go.

5

I COULD HEAR MAMA CRYING softly at night in our small house, and not just because of all that had happened to us. My grandma Fancia's illness was very serious. Aunt Elsa and Mama whispered a lot about her, but would not tell us what was wrong with her.

Silently in bed I would pray that my beloved grandma Fancia would get better, that I would be able to see her just one more time. She was so beautiful, with her delicate face surrounded by white hair piled high in a bun, and she spoke in such a soft, refined voice. I remembered the wonderful times I had with her, sitting on a deep sofa and listening to her tell stories of the Brothers Grimm while I ate pastries and drank lemonade.

I knew that Grandpa Henryk adored her, and I did not know what he would do without her. I missed him too—my tall, straight-walking grandpa with his black mustache. He would talk to Janek and me about such things as love and respect for our elders. Sometimes he spoke about God and about His goodness and wisdom. But I knew I would see Grandpa again, while I was not sure about Grandma Fancia. Only a miracle could save her, I was told, so I prayed for a miracle.

But my grandmother continued to get worse, and then one day we heard the terrible news: she had died in her sleep. We kids were not allowed to go to the funeral. We cried, the mirrors in the house were covered according to custom, and a lot of people visited us. Mama told us that Grandma was better off because she did not have to suffer anymore.

Grandpa Henryk moved in with us; so did Betka, their Jewish cook, who had been with them for thirty-five years and had no other family. But my grandfather had become a different grandpa. He hardly spoke anymore. We tried to cheer him up, and sometimes he would smile. He still loved playing chess with Karol and Janek, and I think that he let them win a few games on purpose, even though he denied it.

All the adults looked sad most of the time now. Food had become hard to get, and new German restrictions and punishments were constantly being posted. But we kids were not unhappy all the time. There was one good thing about the ghetto: we were allowed outside again, though only on our street. We didn't wander away too far; it was dangerous, and we knew it. The trees in our backyard could not protect us; neither could the birds who flew past us. Only our parents could, and this was why we had to listen to them.

It was different playing in the ghetto rather than in the Christian part of town. In a strange way the ghetto was our territory. No one here called us bad names, and there were plenty of kids to play with.

We had a rule: after our evening meal, the children had to go to bed. Aunt Elsa insisted that in our crowded house, the grown-ups needed this time to talk about very important things that could be discussed at no other time.

We kids had fun in the crowded bedrooms. We shared our beds and giggled, whispered, pushed each other and laughed together, hoping the adults in the living room would not hear us. But of course we would also listen in.

We heard that sometimes, risking terrible beatings, the Jewish men and women who were working outside of the ghetto would try to exchange their jewelry or huge amounts of money for meat, butter, or cheese from the Polish people. There were rumors that the Germans were planning to stage a series of "actions," or round-ups, in our part of the ghetto, but no one knew when. They had already made such actions in nearby streets and had taken many women and children away, pulling them out of their apartments or hiding places. Nobody knew where the trucks were taking them. Papa had heard that many of the people were sent to special labor camps in Germany, but no one knew for sure where these were. Sometimes those who were seized were shot instead.

Late at night, Mama and Papa would come to their bed in our room and whisper together in troubled voices. One night, when they thought Janek and I were asleep, I overheard them talking in hushed voices about building a hiding place under our little house. Then Papa spoke about trying to find a home with

Christian friends for me and Janek and our cousins.

I asked him about this the next day. At first he pretended that he didn't know what I was talking about; then he became very upset. "Nelusia, you must promise me that you will not talk with your friends about anything to do with hiding," he said sternly. "It is very dangerous, and it could get us all into a lot of trouble."

I promised that I would not tell anyone, not even Janek. Secretly, though, I didn't believe that such a hiding place could be found for us. How could we even leave for the Polish side of the city? The ghetto was very heavily guarded by the police, and if we were caught outside of it, we would be beaten or shot.

The round-ups began to grow worse: the police were snatching old people, women, and children from the streets and taking them away. Fear ruled with an iron hand inside the ghetto.

My aunt's visa still had not arrived. Sewer was talking seriously with Aunt Elsa about joining the Russian partisans who were conducting a guerrilla war against the Germans from hiding places in the woods.

Only Grandpa Henryk still had faith that things would get better. "Humanity has to awake; this is too painful a nightmare," he said. "We can't exist in this darkness. That is not how God wanted men to live. It has to stop."

I didn't understand Grandpa when he spoke like that of things that I couldn't touch with my hands. Aunt Elsa said he was trying to escape reality, but I wrote some of his wisdom down in my *notatki*, my notes, hoping that one day his words would make sense to me.

6

ONE AFTERNOON soon after our move to the ghetto, in the middle of a freezing rain, the door opened and Mama stormed in. Her clothes and hair were dripping wet.

"Get your coat and hurry, *kochanie* (sweetheart)!" she told me. "There is not much time."

Though I didn't understand what she meant, I quickly put on my coat and kissed Karol, Aunt Elsa, and Ninka. But I didn't want to leave Janek, and I stayed by his side until Mama pulled me away. My last good-bye was to Grandpa Henryk. He hugged me for a long time, looking very sad.

Once outside in the bitter storm, we started to run. I held on to Mama's hand as she kept pulling me faster and faster. We flew through narrow cobblestone streets with deep holes filled with water. Mama did not stop, even when I almost fell into a pothole.

The streets of the ghetto were empty. The rain stung

my eyes and my feet were hurting badly, but Mama kept pulling me on. Even when one of her shoes started to fall apart, she did not slow down—no, she did not. We kept on running until we had crossed the big fields where the pumpkins grew.

"We've passed the ghetto and are in the Aryan part of town," she told me. "Now we must slow down and walk normally. It's dangerous for us to be here, so we can't arouse suspicion."

Luckily, only a few people with umbrellas passed by us. As we walked, Mama explained that I was going to stay with a Catholic family "for a short time—only until the end of the war." I didn't get a chance to ask how long this would be, because she went on to say that Janek would be going away next, as soon as Papa found another Christian family willing to hide a Jewish boy child. (It was harder to disguise the fact that a boy was Jewish, because the Christian boys were not circumcised.)

We reached Wołynska Street without being stopped by the police. Soon we entered a dark hallway and climbed narrow steps to a second-floor corner apartment—the home of the Krajterów family. *Pani* Krajterowa was waiting there in the living room.

I remember feeling very sad as Mama kissed me good-bye; then I started to cry. I wanted her to stay with me a little bit longer. She promised that we would all be together again soon and kept repeating that I must listen to what *Pani* Krajterowa told me. She held me very close for a few minutes and kissed my cheek before she opened the outside door and disappeared into the dark corridor.

After Mama left, I felt lonely and unhappy. The room looked terribly strange to me with all the holy pictures of Jesus and Mary on the walls. But *Pani* Krajterowa opened her arms and hugged me. She told me that she liked me and that I was now to become Marysia, her niece from a small and distant village.

"You don't have the necessary false documents to show that you are a Catholic girl, but you have nothing to worry about," she said in a soothing voice. "Just remember your new name is 'Marysia,' and try to become a truly good Catholic in case someone should suspect something and start asking questions."

The next day, *Pani* Krajterowa started to teach me about the Catholic religion. I learned prayers and the catechism and heard stories from the New Testament. The best part of this new religion was the tales about the holy mother of God's miracles. I also loved to look at *Pani* Krajterowa's holy porcelain figures, which shone beautifully. I was allowed to dust them anytime I wanted to.

Both *Pan* and *Pani* Krajterowie were good to me and encouraged me to call them "Aunt" and "Uncle." Uncle Krajter brought me picture books—in case I got bored, he said—and they tried to keep me laughing with their jokes. I liked them, especially Aunt Krajterowa, and maybe because of that I started to enjoy my new religion and to learn the prayers quickly.

Still, the apartment was very quiet. Hardly anyone ever visited. I knew that was why Mama and Papa had placed me there, but I was very lonely. The days passed by slowly, and sometimes I felt as if I would never see my family again. I wanted to go back home to the ghetto, where I belonged.

Once a week I wrote a little note to Papa, which Uncle Krajter would deliver to him in the factory. They met weekly for "some living arrangements" (which I only later understood to mean payment for keeping me). Sometimes Papa wrote back; other times, he would just tell Uncle Krajter to explain to me that I had to be patient and wait "a bit longer."

And so I waited. At night I tried to forget my sadness by pretending that Janek was in bed beside me. I would tell him the scary story about the witch Baba Yaga, with her house that stood on chicken legs, or about one-eyed Vladimir the cat, who walked like the Czar until a peasant sewed him up in a sack and threw him into the forest. But with the early morning, my make-believe world would vanish and I would be alone again.

I kept asking Aunt Krajterowa if I could go outside just once, and she gave in at last. I couldn't wait to join the neighborhood children, who always gathered on the long interior porches, the *ganki*, facing the backyard of the five-story apartment building.

On that wonderful afternoon, *Pani* Krajterowa walked me to the door, reminding me once again that I was her niece. For the next few days, I played with many children and had fun—until one day, a new little boy came over to join us. He was very small, almost like the Lilliputians in my book *Gulliver's Travels*, and he stuck his tongue out at me.

From that day on, everything changed. Suddenly, I don't know why, the boy hit me and I hit him back. I didn't mean to get into a fight; I'd forgotten who and where I was, until I was reminded.

A woman leaned out from a window above us,

pointing her finger at me. "Jew kid, you hit my child. How dare you, *Żydowska świnia* (Jewish swine)!" she shouted.

Terribly scared, I ran back to the apartment in tears and told Aunt Krajterowa, who dropped the glass bowl she'd been holding and turned white. But when she saw how frightened I was, she hugged and kissed me and didn't even scold.

"I'll take care of everything," she promised, crossing herself and then kneeling before the holy picture of the Madonna and the baby Jesus. It was all very frightening, and I knew then that I would never again go outside to play. I prayed too that the angry *Pani* would not go to the Gestapo and report me.

For days, we listened carefully for any new footsteps or other signs of danger in our hallway. I'd heard that Jews posing as Christians were in greater danger of being discovered by Poles and Ukrainians—who could recognize the Jewish people more quickly—than by the Germans, who didn't have the same understanding of Polish speech, manners, and dialect that the natives did. Some were tempted by the money that was offered for any information about Jews; others, perhaps, turned us in as a way of expressing their hatred for us.

The Gestapo did not come to get us, and by the end of the week I had stopped imagining what might happen to me if they did. Such thoughts were too scary to dwell on.

About two weeks later, on a cold and sunny day, Uncle Krajter came rushing into the apartment, so panic-stricken that he could hardly speak.

The Germans, he told us, were going from door to

door, searching every house, because it was rumored that some Jews were hiding in the neighborhood. They had already started to search our street! I was horrifed and certain that they would come and shoot us all down; Christians who hid Jews were punished the same way as those they had tried to protect.

I could not stop crying as Aunt Krajterowa nervously tried to push me under the bed, pulling the bedcover down to the floor. A few minutes later, she decided that I should hide in a closet instead, and I crawled out. Finally, they said that I should stay in the bedroom and pretend to play with my doll.

I sat on the bed and they sat down with me, trying to talk me out of my fear. I knew that I couldn't pass for a Catholic girl with my black, frightened eyes and dark pigtails; the police would recognize me immediately. I didn't even speak a village dialect, as "Marysia" would; my language was one of a city.

Minutes walked by with small steps. I prayed in silence very hard, holding my doll in my arms. *Pan* and *Pani* Krajterowie knelt next to me, begging God to save us. I couldn't swallow; my throat was too tight. Then the miracle happened! The Germans checked every other house on the street, but missed ours.

When the danger had passed, Aunt Krajterowa began to cry, repeating that my life had been spared by a miracle. She thanked Maria, mother of God, and asked me to join her in prayer on my knees beside her. After our prayer, Aunt Krajterowa told me about the many other wonders that Maria had performed in the past. Every year, she said, more and more people made the pilgrimage to our beloved city of Częstochowa, the famous religious center where *Matka Boska Często-chowska* (Our Lady of Częstochowa) would grant one's wishes.

I agreed that it was a miracle that the Germans should miss only our apartment building out of the *whole block*. Yet I was not sure if it was God's miracle, or the work of *Matka Boska Częstochowska*. I would have to talk to Papa and Mama about that, I decided.

That night, as I lay in bed, I cried for them again. I prayed that God wouldn't think I was ungrateful, considering that He had saved my life. I thought about my shortcomings and wondered whether, if I changed, I would be reunited with my family sooner. But how could I change? Could He tell me? Guide me?

From that day on, every morning and night, Aunt Krajterowa would kneel with me in front of the picture of the Mother of God that hung in a beautiful gold frame above the bed she shared with Uncle Krajter. We would pray aloud to Maria—not to Jesus, her son, even though he was God. I did not understand why this was so but did not ask.

7

Life with the Krajterów family changed again with the arrival of our new boarder, a *Panna* Wanda.

"She is a nice girl, a secretary," Uncle Krajter assured me. But still, Aunt Krajterowa reminded me, I was not to forget that I was their Catholic niece from the country. "Don't slip, don't make a mistake, just remember you are my niece."

I would repeat to myself, "Niece, niece, niece! A niece from the village." My learned grandpa Henryk, who had taught me to read and write, used to say that before going to bed was the best time to memorize something of importance, so that was when I would practice.

I was scared when I finally met *Panna* Wanda. She was tall and blond with a tight, pursed mouth; she did not smile. I was so afraid that I would make a mistake and expose myself that I hardly spoke to her.

She moved her clothes into my closet, ate her breakfast with us, then left for work, and I didn't see her again until the evening meal. But during the day, *Panna* Wanda's shadow was with me. I could feel it watching me, dark, dangerous, and mean.

I made sure to leave the door to the bedroom open at night when I knelt and crossed myself in front of the picture of the mother of God, so that she would see my devotion. But even in bed I could sense her shadow grinning at me.

If only *Panna* Wanda did not have to live with us! I tried to stay out of her way as much as I could, but I sensed her watching me carefully. Did she already know the truth? Would she go to the police? Or would she demand money from Papa for keeping quiet? I had heard a story from Uncle Krajter about a neighbor of theirs who blackmailed a Jewess who had Aryan papers, took her money, and then went to the police anyway to turn in her and her little boy. The Gestapo picked up both of them. Would *Panna* Wanda do the same? What would happen to me then?

One day Aunt Krajterowa whispered to me that her sister, *Pani* Zosieńka—my "mother"—would soon be coming to visit us. "You must be prepared to act as though she is really your mama," she told me.

The next evening, after a little knock on the front door, a heavyset woman in a black print dress arrived. Uncle Krajter ran over and greeted her in a nervous voice while Aunt Krajterowa came behind my chair and gave me a push.

For a brief moment, I wasn't sure what to do, but then I remembered. I ran toward this strange woman, put my arms around her neck, and kissed her. I could feel *Panna* Wanda's eyes glued to my back, piercing right through my blouse. Silently I prayed that *Pani* Zosieńka would remember that I was supposed to be her daughter. She did. She kept kissing me, and I knew that we were both playing a game for *Panna* Wanda's eyes.

My "mother" and I had to share the same bed. That night, *Pani* Zosieńka told me about her three daughters and a son, who lived with her and her husband on a big farm with pigs, cows, and chickens. They had dogs and cats too. "My animals are much smarter than people; they are not as mean," she told me.

I liked *Pani* Zosieńka. She was friendly and sweet, and tried to make me feel less scared by telling me funny stories about the daily jobs everyone in her family had to do. But when *Panna* Wanda came home from work, I became nervous again and called *Pani* Zosieńka "Mama" too many times in a loud voice.

I was happy when my new mother finally left after a few days, because I did not have to pretend anymore. I was very worried about *Panna* Wanda. I did not think she had believed our charade, because her eyes followed me around all the time. I wasn't imagining it— or was I?

When I told my fears to *Pan* and *Pani* Krajterowie, they nodded their heads and looked very serious. "You are right. It is too dangerous for you to stay with us any longer," Aunt Krajterowa said sadly. "Yes, it is better for you to leave soon," my "uncle" added, promising to talk to Papa about it.

Two days later, Uncle Krajter brought the wonderful news: Papa had agreed that I should come home.

Sewer was going to meet me and take me to the ghetto.

I was overjoyed when the time arrived to meet my cousin. I kissed my "aunt" and "uncle" and ran downstairs as fast as I could. Leaning against the tall brick building, his black cap pulled down over his forehead, was Sewer. I was all ready to run to him, but he motioned with his head, "no," and I understood.

When I reached him, he told me to just continue walking; he didn't take my hand. I could tell he did not even want me to give him a kiss or a hug. He looked very serious and sad and seemed somehow older. Feeling hurt, I walked next to him with quick steps, trying to keep up, shivering in my coat against the cold wind.

Sewer whispered to me that we must not draw attention to ourselves. We were "outside," on the Aryan side, far from the ghetto, and we'd have to blend in with the crowd or else we would get caught.

It was best not to talk at all, he said, but to pay attention where we crossed the street and avoid the corners where policemen were standing. If we were caught by the Gestapo, they would shoot us, he warned me.

I couldn't wait to hear all the news about Janek, Ninka, and Karol, and I asked Sewer about them. He answered firmly that I would have to wait till we got to the ghetto. Then he changed his mind and told me that they were all fine, but that now was not the time to talk about it. "Later," he said.

"But how is Janek?" I kept insisting, and he repeated, "Fine, fine—not now."

There was something strange and frightening about

the way Sewer answered. "What's wrong?" I asked, but Sewer just shook his head and told me again that this was not the time to discuss it. I'd have to wait until we left this section of town.

It was in the ghetto that he told me the terrible news. They came and took them . . . Ninka, whom Aunt Elsa had hidden under the bed; Janek, who was squeezed behind a chest of drawers, and my aunt. She had pleaded for the children, but they took them all and did not listen to her cries. Aunt Elsa showed various documents to the Gestapo man, but he only laughed and then ripped them all up. She fell on her knees and begged them to leave the children and take her instead, but the Gestapo and the Ukrainian policemen just shouted angrily at her. Then the Ukrainian slapped her face . . . and they took them all.

Karol watched everything through a keyhole in a closet. He watched everything . . . then he ran for miles to Papa's factory to see if anything could be done, if we could somehow get them off the train. But it was too late—they were already on it.

This was Sewer's dreadful news. Janek, Ninka, and Aunt Elsa were gone, and all my tears could not bring them back.

When I reached home, Mama and I hugged and kissed for a long time, and we cried. I was home at last, but it was not the same. Emptiness filled the crowded rooms.

In the days that followed my return, I half-convinced myself that Janek might somehow have escaped. Maybe he had jumped off the train; maybe a peasant had helped him, and Ninka and Aunt Elsa too. Maybe they were all hiding somewhere in the woods with the partisans, waiting for the end of the war. When I told Mama my thoughts, she quickly said that miracles do happen. Grandpa Henryk, always hopeful, echoed her: "*Cudy* (Miracles) happened many times in the Bible."

Everything had changed since that terrible day. The sky in our town seemed always dark. Even the ants, usually so busy in the loose dirt in front of our little house, seemed to have moved on to someplace better. Nights were the saddest time for me; that's when I missed Janek the most.

Sewer tried to spend a lot of time with Karol and did everything to cheer up his brother, but he could not. Nor could Mama, Papa, Grandpa Henryk, or I. Karol would not talk about Aunt Elsa or Ninka to anyone. He did not cry; he was just very quiet, and his eyes looked even bigger than usual behind his black-rimmed glasses.

Mama said we were lucky that I had not been home. Had I been with Aunt Elsa, I too would have been taken away.

As Mama spoke, I tried not to stare at her newly dyed hair. She was trying to look like a Polish Gentile, but unfortunately her hair had turned bright red instead of blond, as she had intended. She was going to try to dye her hair blond again, since that was the safest shade—but once the war was over, Mama told me, she would go back to her own brown color.

8

SOON AFTER MY RETURN to the ghetto, Mama shared with me an important secret: she and I were going to escape from Lwów together. The rest of the family would follow later, she said, but she didn't tell me where we would be going. I was not allowed to talk to anyone about it; someone could denounce us. And so I didn't say anything to my best girlfriend, Lusieńka, and even Sewer and Karol did not know about our plans until the last day. The fewer people who knew, the safer we were.

We all hugged and kissed good-bye. I held in my tears when Karol squeezed me tight, just as Sewer tried his best to look cheerful even though his sad smile betrayed him. Grandpa held me for a long time in his arms, and then the door closed behind us.

We left on a cold, windy winter day. Only when Mama and I had left Kleparowska Street did she tell me that we were escaping to Hungary. *Pan* Blaustein, my friend Maryla's father, had organized the trip. He knew an important German major who was going to lead us—along with a group of other people—out of Poland to a Hungarian border village. We were on our way to the Blausteins' apartment house on the other side of the ghetto, where Papa would be waiting with a suitcase for us.

"We will pretend to be the major's laborers, doing special projects for him in the fields of Szezelczyska village," Mama explained.

"But what will happen if we're found out?" I wanted to know.

"We will not be caught," Mama said. "We paid lots of money for the major's guarantee. He will get us safely across the border, and there's nothing to worry about."

After a long walk, we finally reached the Blausteins' apartment building. It was late afternoon; a metal lamppost on the corner threw a dim light on the building, number 29.

We entered a crowded room filled with smoke. Papa was talking with a young woman near the window.

Pan Blaustein stood with his wife and two daughters, Maryla and her fourteen-year-old sister, Rózieńka. He was explaining to the people gathered around him that they were coming with us too.

"That's why it is safe," I heard an older man tell a lady. "He wouldn't put his own family into danger."

Maryla and I found a table in the kitchen and started playing cards. People around us formed little groups. They talked very fast, moving their hands nervously and looking serious.

Mama came over to reassure me that Karol, Sewer,

and Papa were to join us later. "In the meantime, your father will try to find hiding places for *Babcia* Tyncia, Grandpa Josef, Aunt Regina, and Grandpa Henryk," she said. "Then he will join us, and we'll all be together again."

I nodded, trying to take all of this in. Mama added that I wouldn't have to be afraid anymore, because it was much safer to be in Hungary than in Poland.

As it grew darker outside, everyone started to get ready. Then we all rushed downstairs, toward a small truck parked in front of the building. Each of the adults carried a little suitcase similar to ours, or a knapsack.

Papa walked with us briskly to the truck, which was covered with a tarpaulin cloth roof. When he put his arms around me, I would not let go of him. He gave me a last kiss and pushed me up into the narrow dark space in the back of the truck. Mama followed.

As the last people squeezed in, we had to lie on top of each other to fit everyone inside. Almost immediately, the motor started with a roar and we drove off with great speed, traveling over bumpy roads. The truck shook a lot, but no one complained.

After a while, I began to feel water dripping on me. It had started to rain, and there was a hole in the truck's roof right over my head. I tried to move to another spot, but I couldn't, squashed between all the legs and arms. Mama somehow managed to cover me with her coat, though it didn't help much.

It seemed like a long ride. I must have dozed off, and I didn't wake up until the truck came to a stop in the darkness of the deep forest surrounding us.

We were not too far from the village of Jagoryce, according to our driver, who quickly drove off into the silent night as soon as we had gotten out. Holding Mama's hand tightly, I followed *Pan* Blaustein along with the rest of the group.

It had stopped raining, but the ground was still so wet and muddy that my shoes would occasionally sink into the cold earth. We walked for a long time through clusters of trees, until finally we stopped in front of an empty wooden barn.

Pan Blaustein opened the unlocked door and we went in. Everyone gathered bunches of the straw piled in the corner of the barn to make up beds on the cold floor. I could feel the prickly straw penetrating through my clothes for only a few minutes; then I fell asleep.

When we woke up, the bright sun was shining through the thick forest. I met Ewka, a girl my age whom I liked right away, and we became friends. She too was there with only her mother. Mama recognized a couple of people she had known before the war, and she seemed satisfied to see some familiar faces. I counted our group; there were twenty-three of us in all.

We spent the day in the barn talking quietly, eating the food we had brought in our suitcases, and waiting for further instructions. That evening, *Pan* Blaustein told us that he had received a message from the German major that we had to move on. In the middle of the night, protected by the darkness, we started toward Szezelczyska.

We climbed over slippery hills and passed through thick forest land, following *Pan* Blaustein. At last he led us to the outskirts of the sleeping village; we could see its narrow streets lined with thatched houses. We crossed a barren patch of land and reached our destination: a big, empty milk barn that stood alone in the middle of a field.

Inside, narrow wooden boards piled with hay were stacked up along the walls. Again Mama made us a bed of hay on the floor and covered me with it to keep me warm. My feet were very thankful as I fell asleep.

Early the next morning, when Mama was still sleeping, I suddenly woke up, sure that I had heard voices outside.

From my bed I could see only the sky, still a dark grayish-purple. Then I heard the whispers again and I knew I was not dreaming. There were people outside our barn.

I got up and moved slowly on my hands and knees to the uncovered opening in the wall that served as a window. Peeking out, I saw a group of peasants carrying farm tools and sticks as they approached our door.

Quickly I woke up Mama, and soon everyone else was up too. Now the peasants had surrounded our building, talking loudly in Ukrainian and Polish dialects. Just as *Pan* Blaustein shouted to us to move back from the window, a stone fell in, followed by a few more. Then everything happened very quickly.

A tall blond boy jumped through the window and grabbed *Panna* Lusia's hand; he yelled that he wanted her watch. She screamed, and *Pan* Blaustein took out a bundle of *złoty* from his pants pocket and gave it to the young peasant. He took the money but would not let go of *Panna* Lusia's hand. The other peasants waited outside, still shouting. Finally *Panna* Lusia's brother ordered her to listen to the boy, and with trembling hands she gave him the gold watch.

Pan Blaustein, looking very angry, went outside and spoke to the peasants near the door. He told them that we were a labor group working for an important German major, and that he would report them and make a lot of trouble if they didn't leave. They cursed at us, but then turned around and walked away.

Only later, after they were gone, did Mama tell me that *Pan* Blaustein had been quite scared, and had just pretended to be angry. "God knows what would have happened if they had all stormed inside our barn," she said.

From then on, the peasants and their children often came near our open window and stared at us. Sometimes they called us "filthy Jews" or threatened to beat us up. Of course, I was not allowed outside without an adult, and neither were Ewka, Maryla, or Rózieńka. But we would not have gone anyway; we were too frightened.

After we had been in Szezelczyska for a couple of weeks, the peasants seemed to have satisfied their curiosity about us and stopped coming by to harass us; instead they came to barter. I could see the hate in their eyes and hear the curse words muttered under their breath as they exchanged their goods with us. They sold us still-warm cow's milk, goat cheese, sweet butter wrapped in brown leaves, cabbage, eggs, potatoes, beans, and red beets. In return they took our money, or our gold and jewelry, which they liked even better.

My diary. Written on the front is
Moje Przeżycia—"My Life."

The first page of my diary; I titled it "Under Occupation, Chapter I,
Beginning of Barbarism, 1941." The small picture illuminating the *P*
shows the Germans marching into Lwów. Although I had taken notes
(my *"notatki"*) about these events at the time they occurred, when I was
six, I did not develop them into this journal until I went into hiding in
1943 at the age of eight. This explains two small errors that readers of
Polish might note on this page: The Germans entered Lwów at the end of
June, not July 21 as I stated, and the yellow armbands were to be worn by
those fourteen and over, not twelve as I had remembered here.

Talking With Mother in the Green Salon · This painting reflects the colors and furniture of the drawing room in our apartment before the war.

All Alone · I made up a story in which a girl has to take a trip by herself; she is lonely. This is how I felt when my parents placed me with the Krajterów family.

Mother, Governess, and Mother's Three Children · My brother and I had a tall governess whom I liked very much, and I remembered the walks we used to take together in the park before the war.

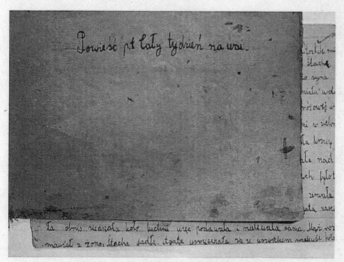

The cover and part of a story from the booklet that I called "Week in the Country." Based on our attempted escape to Hungary, the seven paintings showed happy peasant villagers going about their daily activities. Our real experience with the peasants of Szezelczyska was terrible; they tried to kill us.

Peasant Villagers and Their Daily Activities · From "Week in the Country."

Washing Clothes · From "Week in the Country."

Going to Church · From "Week in the Country."

Sunflowers Growing in the Shadows · We hid in a swamp like this one during our attempted escape to Hungary.

A Trip With Father: A Present for Good Behavior · This picture and the two that follow were part of a booklet I called "Happy Gentleman Farmer"; they were another contrast with my real life.

Girl With Father · In reality I kept waiting for my father to arrive.

Children Walking · While in hiding I was not able to go outside and take walks, so I imagined them in my mind and painted them in my pictures.

A Walk With Teacher · This and the next two watercolors are from the booklet I called "School and Punishment."

History Class · The board reads *Król August*—"King Augustus"—though I do not recall what that meant in my story. The notation "29 VII 1943" indicates that I completed this painting on July 29, 1943.

Being Punished at School · This shows a little girl being punished in the principal's office. She hangs her head, ashamed.

We no longer depended on *Pan* Blaustein, who went to see the major in town weekly, to bring us food; all we needed from him was the news from the German. As the weeks went by, Mama and the others in our group became nervous and started to question him. Why were we waiting here so long? Would we ever get to Hungary? But *Pan* Blaustein assured us that the major was not ready yet; we just had to wait for the right moment before moving on.

We had no choice but to be patient, and so we waited. Most of the people in our group were friendly, and we got to know each other well in the long days we spent together. I especially liked *Pan* Max, *Panna* Lusia's brother, a cheerful bachelor with a big belly who kidded around and told many jokes. He was always with *Pan* Arthur and *Pan* Szulin; they were called "The Three Musketeers."

Pan Arthur, who was respected by most of the adults for his intellect, was "the advocate" because he tried to settle various fights and arguments. *Pan* Szulin, who would often sit in the corner and write his poetry by the dim light of a naphtha lamp, before it grew too dark to see, was "the poet." Sometimes he spoke to us girls in a very serious, grown-up way. There were rumors in our barn that *Pan* Szulin had lived in Moscow before the war and was a "big fish" with the Communists, but no one spoke openly about this since belonging to the Communist Party was frowned upon.

We had been in Szezelczyska about four weeks when *Pan* Blaustein rushed back from town extra early with a new plan. The major had said we must separate into small groups and move on to nearby villages "for safety reasons." Once we were there, we would wait two weeks for *Pan* Blaustein to come and get us. Then we would be reunited for our final trip to the Hungarian border.

No one liked the idea of this separation, and the room filled with angry voices. *Pan* Blaustein stayed calm as he explained that by dividing into smaller groups, we would arouse less suspicion among the peasants. They would be told that we were traveling to work on a special project assigned by the German major.

Still no one had confidence in this plan. Many raised their voices and began to shout; a few ladies covered their faces with handkerchiefs and burst into tears. But *Pan* Blaustein insisted that he could not change the major's orders. We had no choice but to break up, he said.

He drew up a list of those who would have to leave. The next day, this transfer sheet was completed and he started to call off the names. Ours were on the list.

But Mama was firm: she refused to go. She told *Pan* Blaustein that we absolutely would not leave Szezel-czyska unless his family did too. Though *Pan* Blaustein's face turned red with fury at Mama's opposition, we stayed, together with a handful of others: Ewka, her mother, *Pan* Max and his sister, the Blausteins, and a friendly young man named *Pan* Adaś, who looked like a Gentile with his blond hair. The others left in tears.

The days were slowly passing by, and there were no new messages from the major. *Pan* Blaustein kept assuring us that we would be starting for the border soon if we could only be patient.

By now the peasants were happy enough with the

exchange of goods that they no longer threatened to beat us up. When they came to our barn, usually in groups, they seemed less angry. I wondered if one day they might actually stop hating us.

Early one Sunday morning, just two peasants walked to our barn—a handsome young boy with a pretty, blond, rosy-cheeked, pigtailed girl. They were dressed in their Sunday best, festive Polish country clothes, and wearing good shoes for the special occasion of going to church. She wore a clean white blouse and a colorfully embroidered camisole under her open sheepskin coat, and the young man, also in a sheepskin, wore well-polished shoes and a big black hat that covered his head. Both were carrying large baskets filled with brown and white eggs and jugs of milk.

The girl smiled at me as I stood next to Mama, who was concluding a transaction. Then they headed down the narrow road leading to the village church. Other peasants joined them. The church bells started to ring and the sun came out as they began singing hymns to *Matka Boska,* Mother of God.

Their voices carried the melody through the quiet fields. I watched them until they disappeared down the windy path, feeling suddenly jealous. I too wanted to go outside in the sun and not be afraid. I reminded myself of the words that *Pan* Szulin had told me one day when I was feeling sad: "We'll have a big party once we arrive in Hungary. We just have to wait a bit longer."

A week later, when *Pan* Max decided to take a trip to a milk farm that was supposed to be not too far from us, Maryla and I were able to convince our mothers to let us go with him. It was wonderful to run through the empty fields and stretches of small forests, kicking dead branches and braiding crowns from the dried-up yellow and brown flowers. Holding hands, we climbed little hills and saw in the distance thatched-roof farms that looked like toy houses.

We passed a half-frozen freshwater stream where three women were washing clothes, and came to a big red barn. *Pan* Max knocked, and we waited until we were told to come in.

Two women in long dresses covered by caftans were inside, milking the cows. The older one offered me sweet milk, still warm from the cow, in a metal cup. Then, for the first time, I saw fresh butter being churned in a wooden barrel. *Pan* Max bought some, along with buttermilk and *śmietana* (sour cream)—"the best in all Szezelczyska," said the younger woman.

Back outside, birds flew past us as we walked to our barn. We passed a peasant girl pumping buckets of water and ice from a well and came back feeling happy and peaceful, our faces burning from the wind and sun.

Our parents would now allow Maryla, Ewka, and me to go outside to play as long as we stayed right near the barn. Sometimes Rózieńka came too. We were ecstatic at being able to play catch and hopscotch again, run around the building, or just sit near the door to talk or softly sing our favorite songs. Sometimes we stuck pea pods on our noses to look funny, or arranged dried leaves into bouquets as gifts for our mothers. Other times we simply watched the slow-moving clouds and the flocks of blackbirds until we were called in at dusk for our evening meal.

This was cooked on a little kerosene stove that stood in the corner of our barn. It was fun to listen in on the adults' chatter, everyone seated on long wooden benches to eat the steaming hot potatoes, carrots, and boiled cabbage that we had bought from the peasants. When it grew dark, we all went to sleep. As I cuddled up next to Mama, I forgot how uncomfortable my hay bed was.

One afternoon, as the sun fought to break through threatening clouds, *Pan* Blaustein rushed back from his weekly trip to town looking pale and scared. Shaking, he told us about the latest rumor: the Germans were planning to make a surprise "action" very soon to "clean" the local villages of the remaining Jews. To make matters worse, our major had left town suddenly, and no one knew where he could be found. Now there was no one to protect us.

Panic spread through the barn. Rózieńka started to cry, and so did Ewka. She couldn't find her mother, who had gone to town and was probably still there.

Pan Max grabbed Ewka's and *Panna* Lusia's hands, and Mama took mine. Together we started to run toward the woods, the Blausteins and *Pan* Adaś ahead of us.

We flew through the fields and narrow back roads, finally slowing down near a swamp where sunflowers grew in the shadows of tall trees. It was a good hiding place, *Pan* Max said, and we decided to stay.

Whispering to one another, we huddled together on the wet earth and waited. At first, silence cloaked us, but when it had grown dark, we suddenly heard shooting in the distance. The crows descended in huge groups, flying low over our heads and cawing loudly. Were they looking for dead flesh? Through the harsh sounds of the crows we could hear the shots getting closer. Ewka kept sobbing softly, begging us to let her go look for her mother. We would not let her out of sight. Crouching on the cold ground, afraid to cough or move, we waited for hours, praying that we would not be discovered.

About twelve o'clock that night, *Pan* Blaustein and *Pan* Adaś decided to sneak back into the village to see if the major had returned or sent some kind of message. And so they left.

We listened to the voices and sounds of the swamp. I do not know how long we stayed there, motionless. The shooting had stopped; now we could hear only the echoes of the crows and the distant voices of the peasants. Then, suddenly, we heard a scream—a woman's voice piercing the darkness—followed by the loud cry of a baby and a shot. This time the sound was much closer to us.

Mama held me tight. My terror made breathing difficult. Suppose I had to cough . . . could I choke it back? The Germans were very close, somewhere to the left of where we hid. We listened for their footsteps or any other suspicious sounds, but we could hear only the vicious crows and the voices of the swamp.

The hours dragged on; we waited. The dark sky lifted and it started to get light, but *Pan* Blaustein still was not back. His wife began to cry, sure now that the Germans had killed her husband. Ewka continued trying to convince us that she should leave us. Mama tried to assure her that her mother was hiding some-place in the woods, that we would all be reunited soon if only we waited till the "action" was over. But Ewka just kept on crying softly.

Suddenly we heard the branches move. I grabbed Mama's hand. Then I saw *Pan* Adaś. He looked terrible.

"The 'action' is all over," he said. "As far as we know, the Germans killed all the Jews left in the nearby villages, including our whole group."

Nobody spoke as *Pan* Adaś struggled to collect him-self.

"*Pan* Blaustein is waiting for us back at the barn," he said. "We can go back now; it's all over. There are no signs of the major," he added. "He has disappeared."

So we were the only ones who were still alive. The rest were gone. The villages had indeed been "cleaned out"—made *Judenfrei*, Jew-free.

"No one has heard yet from Ewka's mother," he said gently, putting his arm around Ewka. She was now crying uncontrollably, and we all huddled close to her as we started to walk back to the barn, very quietly.

Pan Blaustein met us outside the barn. The place was in shambles; all our belongings were missing. Our beds of hay had been kicked around, and the whole place looked as if angry dogs had rampaged through it.

Later that morning *Pan* Blaustein went to see the sheriff about our missing luggage; he gave him money, and a few hours later the peasants returned most of the suitcases. They threw them against the side of the building, spitting, cursing, and shouting that they were sorry we had not been killed too.

That afternoon, Papa heard what had taken place in Szezelczyska. He came to get us in a small car driven by a German officer, whom he had paid "generously," according to Mama. We headed back to Lwów, and so did *Pan* Blaustein, who was able to get a truck for his family, Ewka, *Pan* Max, *Panna* Lusia, and *Pan* Adaś. Ewka would have a sad reunion with her father in the ghetto.

Everyone knew by now that the trip to Hungary had been a hoax, only to get money from us. The major had fooled us all.

9

WE DIDN'T GO BACK to our house on Kleparowska
Street right away. Papa was afraid that someone might
have found out that we'd tried to escape and reported
us to the Gestapo. Instead, we went to my mother's
great-aunt Hanna's house.

I did not know this aunt well and can only remember three things about her. She had a grown son; her
husband had been shot by the SS; and she had a special
ring with a green stone in which she kept cyanide—
poison—"just in case," as I overheard her say to Mama.

After we had stayed with Aunt Hanna for a couple
of days, Papa decided that it was safe for us to return
to our house. We went back to Kleparowska Street on
an angry, windy day with a biting chill that penetrated
right through my coat. Nothing had changed much
there. Our small bungalow, its narrow windows covered with icicles, still faced the same, muddy river
Płtew. Its sluggish waters were partially frozen over,
and I can remember watching the chunks of ice on the

river move slowly away from the ghetto and wondering if they were escaping to a better place.

Our little house still breathed of Janek, Ninka, and Aunt Elsa. At night I thought I could hear my little brother whispering from behind the goose-feather pillow. Sometimes I dreamed that Janek was telling me not to be afraid, that he was coming home soon and that we would be together again.

I awoke to a bleak reality. The streets were empty most of the time. People with sad and sunken faces walked to work under police escort. No one smiled; no one looked up.

I found two of my girlfriends, Sonia Fruch and Zula Pomeranz, still living across the street with their parents. Pretty Sonia, with her big blue eyes and thick black braids even longer than mine, and Zula, who was quiet and shy, were happy to see me again.

The first couple of days I played with Zula and Sonia, but when Sonia's little brother also wanted to join us, I stopped. They couldn't understand why, and I would not tell them—but Sonia's brother was Janek's age, and whenever I looked at him, I was reminded of my sweet Janeczek. From then on, I would only play with my two girlfriends if they came to my house.

Every day Sewer went to work, walking with the group who marched back and forth under guard from the ghetto to the Aryan part of Lwów, and came home very tired. He talked more with the adults now, discussing different ways of escaping; he didn't spend much time with Karol or me anymore. I knew he wanted to get to the woods with Karol and join the partisans. I often heard him say that he would take good care of his little brother and that one day they would go to Australia together, no matter what. Sewer had grown even closer to Mama, who had always adored him.

One day Betka, my grandparents' housekeeper—who was like a member of our family—suddenly vanished in a nearby street during an unexpected round-up. She never returned to our little house again. When I asked Papa what had happened to her, he told me that he had tried to find out where she had been taken but that he could not.

After we had been back on Kleparowska Street for about a month, news came to us in whispers about another "action." It was a quiet, windy Sunday afternoon, and the word passed quickly all along the street: "The Germans are on their way. . . . They are coming. . . ."

We ran to *Pan* Pomeranz's little bungalow, where our neighbor had made a hiding place under his living room. Others had the same idea, and everyone was pushing and yelling.

Pan Pomeranz was going to stay above ground, because he had a "good and safe" working pass from the *Wehrmacht,* the German army. He was already prying up the floorboards when we got there.

"Just children, mothers, and old people," someone shouted.

"Why? Who are you to decide?" yelled back a tall, skinny man whom I did not know.

"Idiot! That's all the Germans are taking today!" screamed *Pan* Pomeranz. "Don't you understand that there is not enough room for everyone?"

The skinny man ran out of the house in a fury, slamming the door behind him.

Mama looked scared as she continued to urge us forward. "Move! Hurry! Nobody stays out! What is the matter with you?" She pushed me behind Karol, who was following Grandpa Henryk.

We all climbed down below floor level and squeezed into a narrow, dark space. Our neighbor, *Pani* Goldfarbowa, clutched her baby close to her and put her hand over the child's mouth. Mama whispered to someone that she hoped the baby would not start to cry and give us all away.

It was so crowded, I could hardly move. A woman's voice was softly complaining about the disaster that the infant could bring upon our heads. "Malka sleeps a lot," *Pani* Goldfarbowa kept repeating. "I will cover her mouth if she wakes up. I'll make sure she is quiet, no matter what I have to do." Then I heard her sobbing softly in the darkness.

The floorboards above us were being pushed back into place, and I could hear the sounds of the hammer nailing them down. A hot, heavy blanket of blackness covered us.

A mouse or rat skittered past my feet. I stumbled up against a stepladder and climbed to the top, my head grazing the low ceiling.

It was hard to breathe; my lips felt very dry. The baby girl, Malka, whimpered, and someone cursed and hissed, "Shut that baby up!"

Mama found me. She managed to climb through all the bodies and sat down on the floor next to the ladder, touching my foot.

There was little air, and I hoped that we would not suffocate. I closed my eyes and tried as hard as I could to think of something less scary, an idea that Mama suggested when things got bad.

I pictured a park with graceful trees full of brown and orange leaves. Janek's white teeth gleamed in the sun as we ran around the bushes, trying to catch a pink and white butterfly. It flew higher and higher into the blue sky. Then, suddenly, a storm descended and thunder shook the air. . . .

It was the boards creaking above us. I heard voices; the Germans were in the apartment.

I jumped down and opened my eyes, straining to see through the blackness. Mama's finger pressed against my lips, warning me to be quiet.

I slipped down onto a friendly lap and felt someone's arm go around me. My throat was as tight as if a rubber band were wrapped around it. Had Janek been this frightened when they came for him?

Then the voices suddenly seemed to move away. We waited in total silence. A door shut with a bang, and it was quiet again. Minutes dragged by, but no one moved. I wondered if this was what eternity was like; Grandpa Henryk spoke of it often as "bottomless."

The floor above us made a whispering sound. Then someone began prying the boards open. I closed my eyes again, not wanting to see who it was.

"It is me. It's all over!" said *Pan* Pomeranz.

We crowded around him. His hands trembled as he spoke, and he kept wiping his forehead.

"When I told the Gestapo that I was alone in the house, they laughed and said they didn't believe me. I

71

watched them pull everything apart, but by some miracle they never lifted this small rug!"

"God watched over us," said Grandpa Henryk, whose hands were shaking also. No one answered him as he continued to pull and twist his dark, neatly groomed mustache. "It will pass soon, this madness. . . . Jews have suffered before. . . ." It seemed as if my grandpapa were talking to himself.

The following day we discovered how terrible the action had been. Whole families were pulled out of their hiding places; they took all the children. Many friends and neighbors whom Mama and Papa knew had been taken; others were shot immediately.

My parents tried their best to shield Karol and me from all the pain and fear raging around us. Like many other adults in the ghetto, they continued to provide educational and cultural experiences for their children, even under those dreadful conditions, to provide some sense of normalcy in our lives.

They engaged a tutor for us—Grandpa Henryk's third cousin, *Pan* Brauss. He was to teach us "proper" reading, writing, and arithmetic, and Karol would also study Hebrew with him.

I took an immediate dislike to this slightly stooped tutor, whose clothes hung loosely on his narrow shoulders. There was something unpleasant about his eyes, which hid behind dirty yellow eyebrows.

He usually ate his midday meal with us, and it was Karol's and my greatest pleasure when he fell asleep at our corner table after a filling meal. My cousin and I made sure we were very quiet then as we played checkers, dominoes, or cards. Sometimes his short, chubby wife would come to pick him up and would become very angry when she found him snoring away.

One day, Karol was sick and I had to have my lesson alone with *Pan* Brauss in the living room. After a few minutes, he stopped in the middle of his reading and asked me if I still collected the dried flowers I had once shown him, pressed neatly between the pages of my Grimm fairy tales. When I told him that, yes, I still did, my tutor promised me a whole bouquet of dried cornflowers wrapped with ribbon if I would take off my underpants and let him look "for just a moment."

I jumped from my seat and started to run as fast as I could from the room. As I rushed toward the door, I heard his voice behind me, urging me to stop—I could have all his colorful pieces of foil from candy wrappers, which he knew I also saved, if I would just wait a moment. I continued to run without pausing until I reached Grandpa Henryk's bedroom; then I fell into his arms and started to cry.

When Grandpa asked me what had happened, I would not tell him. But I refused to see my tutor again, and after a while, Mama stopped trying to persuade me. There were too many other terrible things happening around us now.

First *Babcia* Tyncia and Grandpa Josef "left us forever; they journeyed to heaven," as Papa said. I remember how he stroked my hair when I could not stop crying. I had terrible nightmares for weeks and I would wake up screaming in the middle of the night. Papa tried to tell me that his parents had been lucky to die of natural deaths, in their own beds. It was better that way, he kept repeating. Karol was the one who explained to me that sick and old people were useless to the Nazis because they could not work. Like young children, they were in the greatest danger of being taken away during "actions" or shot down on the spot.

Shortly after, Grandpa Henryk contracted typhus. The typhoid epidemic in the ghetto was rampant; between the food shortages and the fact that there were hardly any Jewish doctors left—all had been taken away—many people died. The crowded living conditions bred the disease.

Food was harder and harder to get. Although it was strictly forbidden, the adults continued to risk their lives to smuggle goods from the Aryan part of town.

The round-ups in the ghetto became more and more frequent. People tried frantically to find hiding spots in the sewers of Lwów, in attics, underground bunkers, or any hole imaginable. As one "action" followed another, those of us who survived seemed to be descending into an inferno of terror.

Then my dear, wonderful Grandpa Henryk died. The adults said Kaddish, but it was too dangerous for us kids to go to the funeral. We cried and stayed home; once again the mirrors were covered.

Papa made a hiding place in the cellar of our house, and during one of the round-ups, when I was ill, Mama lifted me from my sickbed in a panic and rushed downstairs with me. Two little girls were already there with their mothers, along with an old man and young *Pan* Lolek, the cousin of one of my parents' good friends.

In a whisper, this *Pan* told us many frightening stories. At first I could hear his words clearly, despite my throbbing head and throat that felt as if hundreds of needles were piercing it each time I tried to swallow; but after a while they all blended in together.

". . . I was almost caught by local farmers, who were anxious to turn in a Jew for a bag of potatoes and a bottle of vodka," he was saying when I could focus on his words again. "But I made it back to the ghetto, only to find my wife and my baby, my little girl, gone. . . ." His soft cry froze the air in our narrow space.

"Are you asleep?" Mama whispered.

"No." I was awake; my hair felt sticky, and my chest was hurting now as well as my throat.

I heard Mama's voice say, "She has a high fever," to no one in particular.

"I know, I know," someone whispered back.

Mama's arms were wrapped around me. She stroked my hair, and her cool fingers softly touched my wet face. "Go to sleep," she whispered, kissing me.

I felt very, very tired. "Close your eyes, try to sleep. Think of something nice, like a birthday party," she coaxed me. But when I closed my eyes I saw my grandma Fancia's face, the yellow Star of David blowing lightly next to her in the wind and another one whirling down from an ebony sky. Then I saw strange shapes, images from the grown-up stories and myths that Grandpa Henryk used to read to me. An ugly Medusa with hideous snakes writhing in her long hair was moving closer and closer to me. I started to scream, but Mama's hand pressed firmly on my lips. I opened my eyes and then closed them again, feeling secure in her presence. I heard her whisper, "She has fallen asleep, thank God." When I opened my eyes again, the "action" was over.

We surfaced from the cellar. Mama carried me to my bed, where the cool pillow felt as soothing as snow to my hot cheeks. Now beautiful images blossomed behind my closed eyelids. We were all sitting in the living room; Janek, Papa, and I quietly listened to Mama playing a Schubert sonata as Magda walked in, carrying a silver tray filled with pastries and bonbons. Comforted, I fell asleep.

The days following my recovery from this illness seemed to slip by faster and faster in a blur of horror and suffering. One by one our choices were swept away; panic and fear enveloped us.

We no longer lived in our little house on Kleparowska Street; my memory of how we survived has left me. I could not keep my *notatki* during this time, could not record the cruelty and deprivation that were all around us. Thoughts of Lwów's Janowska labor camp, with its shooting, sickness, and death, echoed day and night in my head. Had the world's heart stopped beating?

For endless months, I was aware that each new morning might be my last. One night I had a dream that mirrored the terrible reality of our lives.

I was in Hades, the underworld. Its long, windy corridors ended in doors that were locked and guarded by Cerberus, the monstrous three-headed dog. I knew there was no help from the people of the earth; they had deliberately turned a blind eye to those of us trapped in the endless abyss below.

Then, suddenly, a miracle happened. Someone was pulling me forward, leading me through a strange landscape of broken bodies with silent lips and suffering eyes toward a light ahead. I became aware that it was Grandpa Henryk holding my hand, and he was speaking to me tenderly in the soft, long-ago voice of my memories.

"Don't worry; don't, *kochanie*. I promise it won't last. It's only a bad dream. The darkness will lift; we only have to open that special gate."

A wicked laughter pierced the air of my dream, and a voice hissed, "Listen to this Jewish sage! What is he, some kind of Confucius, still praying for the tolerance of man?" Then, a polite inquiry: "Excuse me, sir, but do you really want to live? It's very difficult, you know, to arrange it. You want fresh air instead of dust filling your lungs? You are asking a lot."

"I know, I know," said Grandpa Henryk. "But there are always little miracles, even when hope has vanished."

This was so like my grandfather—always trying to make me feel better when I was sad, always waiting patiently for the brighter day that he knew was just ahead.

Then came a sunny day in the spring of 1943 when my dream came true—the day that Mama and I escaped.

Part Two
Spring 1943 to September 1944

10

Early on a warm spring morning in 1943, after walking for a long time, Mama and I met Papa at a corner of the park in the Aryan section of Lwów. Our destination was Bajki Street, a fashionable part of town now occupied by many Germans. My father had found a Christian family, the Wojteks, who were willing to risk hiding us.

I followed my parents with my head down, walking alone behind them. It was better this way, Papa said, in case we were stopped. He was not going to be staying with us at the Wojteks'—not until he had found safer hiding places for the boys and Aunt Regina. They were in a temporary hiding place at this point, though I didn't know where. I wished that we could all become invisible, like the air, so the Gestapo would never be able to see us or touch us.

We crossed the street. A long time ago, Janek and I had played in this park with Dana, our governess, who

would bring oranges and bananas and pieces of pine-
apple for us to eat. Now the park was empty; it was
too early for the children to be out.

Mama and Papa were walking faster; I had to hurry
to keep up with them. I only hoped that we would not
be stopped. If this happened, they had told me, I was
to pretend I didn't know them and continue walking
to the address I had memorized on Bajki Street. I had
promised Papa that I would get to *Pani* Wojtkowa's no
matter what happened. "Don't even glance in our di-
rection," he had said, looking very serious. "Just follow our feet and keep up with us."

We left the park. The sidewalk started to fill with
people; two cars drove by, and we passed a tramway.
I tried to keep my eyes on Mama and Papa's moving
shoes.

At last I saw the sign for Bajki Street. We were facing the five-story red brick building where the Wojteks
lived. They had been our tenants before the war; we
had owned this apartment house.

They slowed down, and Papa darted a quick look
around to see if there were any police nearby. Then he
crossed the street and entered the building. He signaled
to us a moment later, and I followed with Mama behind me. We rushed down a dark corridor toward a
half-open door and slipped through it into a kitchen.
The door closed behind us immediately.

A short, stocky woman in a brown calico dress, her
gray hair pinned back on both sides with bobby pins,
smiled at me. Her husband, a stern-looking man with
dark, deep-set eyes, walked out of the bedroom and
kissed Mama's hand, then shook Papa's and mine. His
fingers felt bony and cold.

He motioned to the table and four chairs that stood near the wall. As the adults sat down, Papa pressed an envelope into *Pan* Wojtek's hand.

I looked up at the high ceiling and saw a big cobweb. At one end of the kitchen was a dark bathroom, and at the other, a window reached almost to the floor. Through an open door lay the bedroom. I could see all the furniture inside: two single beds, a sofa, a high metal closet, and a round table with chairs and a mirror above it. A wide green ceramic heating stove decorated with animal shapes rose to the ceiling. These two rooms, the kitchen and the one bedroom, were the extent of the apartment.

Pani Wojtkowa rose and beckoned to me to follow her into the bedroom. There were two windows overlooking Bajki Street, both covered with semisheer curtains. One was over a bed; I went to the other and saw a couple of trees outside and flowers growing in a little front garden surrounded by a wrought-iron fence. When a German in uniform strolled by, I quickly stepped back.

She gave me a cup of light tea and walked with me to the sofa. Papa and Mama were still sitting around the kitchen table, talking with *Pan* Wojtek, and I watched them from the couch. In a moment, *Pani* Wojtkowa joined them again.

Pan Wojtek was frowning; Papa gesticulated with his hands. Mama was biting her lip, and *Pani* Wojtkowa sat motionless, looking at the linoleum that covered the table. I could not hear what they were saying, and slowly their whispers faded away. I felt my eyes getting heavy and dozed off until Papa's kiss on my forehead woke me up.

"I'll be leaving soon," he said, "but first I want to show you your secret window. It's all ready for you."

Papa lifted a colorful kilim rug that hung on the wall near one of the beds, and behind it I saw a small trapdoor. He opened the door to reveal a dark little cubicle.

"This space was once a window," Papa told me, "but it has been bricked over on the street side. It can't be seen from the outside." The windowsill was wide enough for Mama and me to crouch on sideways if we ever needed to hide in there—if anyone should want to see our room.

Papa explained to me how the concealed window came to be. Before the war, *Pan* Wojtek had asked him to cover up one of the three bedroom windows from the outside, to make the room warmer. Knowing how harsh the Polish winters were, Papa had blocked the window off permanently. The bricks blended in with the exterior wall, which faced a building full of high-ranking Germans across the street.

I thought about this coincidence. Had Papa, or the Wojteks, ever imagined that we would have to hide in this secret window? Was it God's hand, as Grandpa Henryk would surely have said?

Once Papa and *Pan* Wojtek had decided to use the window for our emergency hiding space, they had covered the opening with plywood boards to make it look like the rest of the inside wall, then cut out the little door and hung a rug over it. The plan was for Mama and me to stay in the bedroom all the time with the door locked. Only if it should become too dangerous would Mama and I climb into our secret window.

Our day clothes had to be kept inside the cubicle;

Pani Wojtkowa gave us two nightgowns to wear at night. We had to be prepared at all times to climb inside, without leaving the slightest trace behind us. There was always the possibility of a police check or a visit from a neighbor who might want to enter the room for some reason.

Papa suggested a way for *Pani* Wojtkowa to warn us. If anyone should want to come into the locked bedroom, she was to stall, speaking loudly as she walked slowly around the kitchen pretending to look for her keys in the cabinets and drawers. This would give us enough time to get into our window soundlessly. She told us that it was not unusual for people to keep their bedroom doors locked in this expensive section of town; there were frequent robberies.

Mama and I had to practice walking on our tiptoes across the room, stepping carefully on the wooden floor so that it wouldn't squeak, as we made our way to the window. We also had to whisper at all times.

"The walls have ears, and so do the neighbors," *Pan* Wojtek told us. "If someone should suspect us, God forbid, the Gestapo would find us right away! Even without their dogs, they can smell the Jews out!"

He laughed. "But with luck, no one will even dream that Michaj Wojtek would hide Jews. Every Pole knows that they are the cause of all the misery in the world, including Jesus Christ's. What those idiots don't know is that Jesus Christ *was* a Jew! You see, *Pan* Landau, I am not so dumb. I know my religion."

"Of course, of course," Papa responded.

"We are lucky that the apartment has only the one bedroom and is on the ground floor," *Pan* Wojtek went on. "Otherwise the Germans would probably have taken it a long time ago. But without a living room, this place is too small even for the *Volksdeutche*." (These were Polish citizens who had, or claimed to have, a German background.)

He looked at Papa. "Well, *Pan* Landau, remember that there is space in here for you too, even in the window. You can always come to us." My father nodded and thanked him. Mama told me later that he liked Papa a lot.

Then the Wojteks went out, closing the bedroom door behind them and leaving us alone with Papa for a few minutes before he had to leave.

Papa whispered, "I have to show you something important." He walked to the end of the room, knelt down a few steps from the front window, and pried open two floorboards with a little pocket knife. On the sandy ground underneath was a little fabric bag, tied with a string.

"This is where Mama's jewelry is kept." Papa moved closer to me as I stared at the soiled brown package in surprise. "Don't forget; now you know where it is, in case you should ever need it." Mama, standing behind me, looked on intently as Papa pushed the wooden planks back into place.

Then Papa put on his beige jacket and hugged and kissed us for a long time. He went to the kitchen and, after a signal from *Pan* Wojtek, opened the front door swiftly. Then he was gone again.

I kept my tears inside as *Pani* Wojtkowa came into the bedroom. She told me that even though our apartment was close to street level, if I stood far enough from the window, I could look out without being seen.

I hurried over to watch Papa cross the street, walking briskly through the crowd. I only hoped that no one would recognize him; Papa knew many people, and the Ukrainian police were on the lookout for Jews all the time. I prayed for his safety as he disappeared around the corner.

Pani Wojtkowa was in the kitchen clearing the table, rinsing the cups in the sink. When she had finished, she wiped her hands on her apron, and I saw that she had hardly any nails on her fingers and her hands were as wrinkled as *Babcia* Tyncia's. She saw me looking at her and smiled again; I knew right away that I would like her.

Pan Wojtek returned to the bedroom and put on his black hat and galoshes. With a cane in his left hand, he walked over to Mama and kissed her hand. Narrowing his eyes, he looked sternly at me and nodded, then went out.

"I'm afraid of him," I told Mama after he was gone. But she laughed and assured me that I didn't have to worry. This *Pan* was risking his life for us; he was our friend.

As the day stretched on, the apartment began to feel safer to me. I was happy to be with Mama, not alone, as I had been with the Krajterów family. She explained our sleeping situation to me: she and I would sleep together on the bed placed against the wall with the trapdoor. *Pan* Wojtek's bed was the one below a front window, overlooking the street; *Pani* Wojtkowa would sleep on the narrow sofa. I couldn't understand why this was so, when her husband had a big bed—but when I whispered to Mama about this, she told me not to be so nosy.

I watched the normal daily life going on in the street below our windows. Toward late afternoon, it began to rain heavily. On the wide, well-kept avenue, people with umbrellas rushed for shelter, and horses galloped past pulling shiny black *dorożki*.

Absorbed in the sight of boys and girls splashing in the puddles and kicking at the rainwater, I jumped when I heard a sudden knock at the front door. *Pani* Wojtkowa looked in at us with a frightened face before quickly locking the bedroom door. Only then did we hear her open the front door, the one in the kitchen that led out to the corridor. I grabbed Mama's hand, too terrified to breathe. What would happen next? Was this it—did they already know about us?

We stood in the middle of the room like statues, waiting. Then I heard a woman speaking rapidly. Her voice was friendly and she called *Pani* Wojtkowa her "dear *Pani* Krysia"; she must have been a visiting neighbor. She talked and laughed with *Pani* Wojtkowa for what seemed an endlessly long time until finally we heard the sound of her chair being pushed back.

But still she did not leave. Mama and I continued to watch the door and listen, motionless; only my eyes moved around the room. My foot fell asleep, but I did not dare to move it; she was still talking.

At last she said good-bye. We heard the front door close; then *Pani* Wojtkowa came running to unlock the bedroom door. A few minutes later, *Pan* Wojtek walked in, dripping wet. He was holding two umbrellas, one in each hand, over his head, and he looked so funny that I had to cover my mouth so I wouldn't laugh. He bent down and kissed Mama's hand once more.

We ate our evening meal early, before it started to get dark. I knew that it was too dangerous to have the lights on; we would be seen from the street. We moved around in the darkness until bedtime, and our first day in hiding ended without incident.

11

Our new life began to take on a routine. Every morning, after we had washed up, *Pani* Krysia—as we soon began to call *Pani* Wojtkowa—locked our bedroom door and we stayed in there while she went out. When she came back at noon, she would open the door, and we could use the washroom. We didn't dare to use the toilet if no one was home; the neighbors might overhear the water flushing or the footsteps on the linoleum kitchen floor and suspect something. We had to wait until *Pani* Krysia returned.

Pan Wojtek, who was fifty-eight and seemed very old to me, called himself an "emeritus" (retired) mason. He spent his days at the open bazaar, where he bought and sold secondhand clothing: hats, pants, shirts, boots, shoes, jackets, coats, and even watches, umbrellas, and canes. In this cobblestone marketplace, he also sold Mama's jewelry. Of course, he had to go to a different spot each time, so that he wouldn't be asked too many questions. With this money, *Pan* Wojtek bought food and other commodities.

When he came home in the late afternoon, he was often frustrated and tired, but the usual angry expression on his leathery face would brighten when he sat down to tell Mama all about the market. According to him, it was a sort of grown-up playground filled with gossipy, cheating vendors, spies, police, informers, and farmers. Here he bought rhubarb, *poziomki* (tiny wild strawberries), fresh vegetables, yellow butter, and delicious pot cheese wrapped in large green leaves that always smelled of the country to me.

Only meat and chicken were hard to get, though as *Pan* Wojtek said many times, "For enough money, you can get anything." Dog and horse meat were easily available, but we never ate it—at least, I don't think we did, unless someone fooled *Pan* Wojtek into thinking he was buying beef. There were even rumors that there was liverwurst made from Jewish flesh on the market.

I could tell that *Pan* Wojtek liked to be with Mama. After coming to our room, he usually closed the door so his wife couldn't hear him, and spent a long time talking to my mother. He repeated the same stories over and over until I had memorized them. Mama always pretended to be interested, no matter how boring he was. He kissed her hand politely several times a day—"out of respect," he would say.

He was an unpredictable man, and we never knew what kind of mood he was going to come home in. In his crazy way, he was convinced—truly convinced—that his heart had *slowly moved to his right hip*. "It took years for it to slide down like this," he explained to Mama, who nodded her head. "Nobody believes me—only you, a true *dama* (lady), know that I'm telling the truth. That's why I can trust you. The doctors say I'm not normal, can you imagine such a thing?" (This wasn't hard for me to do, but I wouldn't have dared to say so!) "They poked me with special needles to see if I felt any pain, and of course I didn't; it only made my heart beat faster. Only you can understand that, because you, my dear *Pani,* are smart!" Mama continued to nod her head very seriously.

He would take her hand and place it gently on his right hip. "Can you hear my heart beat, *Pani* Landau?" he would ask, and she always said yes, yes, she could. "It's ticking strongly, like a new clock, and I'm proud of it." Mama agreed with him, no matter what he said.

I quickly learned how enraged *Pan* Wojtek could become, so I tried not to laugh at him, but when I couldn't keep it in any longer, I'd go to the farthest corner of the room and turn my face to the wall. Though he was very polite to Mama, and kept telling her how fond he was of the *Pan* and *Pani* Landau, the true *Pan* Wojtek could become very dangerous with his terrible outbursts of temper.

For no reason at all, he would start to hit and shout at poor, wonderful *Pani* Krysia. If he did not like one of her meals, had a bad day, was in a mean mood, or was just trying to "show her who was the boss," he could become wild with fury. He cursed her, called her a tramp and all kinds of insulting names, and threatened to kill her with a hatchet the first chance he got. Sometimes I believed he would really do it, but *Pani*

Krysia told me not to worry; with us watching over her, she was not afraid of "this Lucifer."

Mama always tried to calm *Pan* Wojtek down when he grew violent. Sometimes he would listen, but other times he would just push her away with surprising gentleness. When Mama couldn't stop him, *Pani* Krysia would climb up onto the low windowsill in the kitchen, which faced busy Bajki Street, and start screaming for the police. Then Mama and I would run to the bedroom, crawl into our secret window, and wait, knowing this was the only tool she had to prevent her husband from beating her and hoping that she would stop before the Gestapo came. Didn't he realize what danger he was putting us all in? I often wondered.

One evening, in one of his unexpected fits of temper, he threw a dish of hot fried cabbage *pierogi* (dumplings) right at his wife's face, just missing her eye. The *pierogi,* onions, and lard splattered all over the floor, while *Pani* Krysia screamed and ran into the bedroom.

He picked up a knife and leapt after her, shouting, "I know you and your son are trying to poison me! You can't fool me! You and your son want me dead! I know, I know!"

Mama frantically pushed me to a corner, then ran and placed herself in front of him. She started to reason with him, speaking rapidly, until *Pan* Wojtek dropped the knife. When he began to calm down, she took his hand, led him to the chair, and continued to talk. Since he listened to her, still breathing heavily, I knew that *Pani* Krysia was safe again—for a while.

Of course no one wanted to poison *Pan* Wojtek, but

he was sure that his son, Staś, was behind a plot to kill him. He had thrown Staś out of the house when his son was only seventeen years old and sick with tuberculosis; it had happened during one of his rages. That was ten years before, but even now *Pan* Wojtek said he never wanted to see Staś again. "Not even at my deathbed, I don't want that swine to come near me! He is not mine anyway!"

His wife assured us that Staś was indeed *Pan* Wojtek's real son (I didn't know exactly what she meant by this). We knew that this plot to kill him was all in his head. For years, Staś had had to visit his mother secretly, when *Pan* Wojtek wasn't home; but now that we were hiding there he was no longer afraid. He could easily have denounced us to the police, and *Pan* Wojtek understood that very well.

When Staś knocked three times on the front door to signal that he was coming, *Pan* Wojtek would leave the kitchen right away and enter our room. To calm himself, he would pull out a wooden trunk filled with black, white, and brown beans that he kept under his bed "for the black hour" (in case food became unavailable). Then he would start counting them. Afterward, he would sit and talk with Mama until his son left. We would hear the front door close, and then he would storm into the kitchen, casting ugly looks at his wife.

I never met Staś; I only heard his voice in the kitchen. It was safer that way. I knew a lot about him from his mother, who loved him very much. When she was young, she had run away with baby Stasiek several times to protect him from his father's temper—but since she had no place to go, she always returned.

Years later, after the big fight when Staś was thrown out of his parents' home, he had married a twenty-eight-year-old woman. *Pani* Krysia told us that Ania was "not a poor girl," but unfortunately she died of tuberculosis shortly after the wedding, and seventeen-year-old Staś used up her money. Now he did odd carpentry jobs when he could get them, but still ate his daily meals in his mother's kitchen. Sometimes he worked in the Bajki Street apartment house.

The neighbors in the building were a mixture of Germans and a few Poles. The Polish tenants would never visit *Pani* Wojtkowa when her husband was home. "They hate him," she told Mama. "My smart girlfriend Olga says he is *'nie normalny'* (not normal)."

Pani Krysia had a couple of friends in the building, but this Olga Sociecka was very special. An old tenant, she had known Papa before the war, and one day—after talking it over with Mama—*Pani* Krysia confided to her about us. She explained how bored I was, cooped up inside all day, and asked this *Pani* Olga to do us a favor. I needed something to help keep me busy; could *Pani* Olga get me a small box of water-color paints, a brush, and some small sheets of paper? Or was she too scared?

At first her friend was shocked, then worried: Did *Pani* Krysia know how dangerous it was to hide Jews? But after a few minutes *Pani* Olga said she would buy everything, despite the risk. She didn't have any children; someone might wonder for whom she was buying art materials. People were very nosy—but she was not afraid. She would be cautious and shop in different stores.

Once I started to paint, a new world opened up for me. It was as if the little box of watercolors made a bright path straight through the apartment walls to the outdoors.

When I painted, I was very content and would spend hours on each page. Every scrap of paper was important because I would get only a few pieces at a time. First I drew slowly with my pencil, using my eraser often, before I ever dared to touch my paintbrush to the paper.

Sometimes after I finished my pictures, I would write little stories about the grown-ups and children whom I had painted so carefully. Occasionally I made up stories as I went along, but more often they were in my head even before I began to draw—tales of birthdays, school, dogs, visits with father, or just walks with friends. Then I sewed my artwork and writing together into little booklets and gave them titles. "Growing Up From Kindergarten On," "Week in the Country," and "Happy Gentleman Farmer" were some of my favorites.

In my pictures there was no war, no danger, no police, and no tears. Everyone liked each other in my make-believe land, and all the people were as free as kites in the sky or butterflies in the field. They were like newfound companions to me in my loneliness, and I couldn't wait to take my next walk on paper with my watercolor friends. I almost always showed children together with other children or adults, except for one painting—a portrait that I called "All Alone."

Later on, *Pani* Olga began to get us books from the library. Unlike *Pani* Krysia, she knew how to read, so there wasn't as much danger involved; we hoped no one would suspect that the books were not for her. Each story offered an escape to me, a new journey, and I anticipated *Pani* Olga's book visits eagerly, reading everything she brought. If I didn't understand something, I asked Mama about it.

With the exception of a few authors who wrote for teenagers, most of the books were for adults. I liked Tolstoi's beautiful writing, but found it harder to understand than another Russian writer, Gorki. Dostoyevski made me ask a lot of questions; I couldn't always follow Goethe; Balzac was too involved and detailed; and Alexandre Dumas, with his heroic battles, was very exciting. But my favorites were the adventure stories of Jack London, Jules Verne, and Karl May. Even though May had never set foot in the United States, his American Indians moved, fluidly and silently, through my imagination.

Harriet Beecher Stowe's *Uncle Tom's Cabin* made me angry. I couldn't believe the way the white men had treated their slaves! Although I had never seen any black people, I hoped someday to meet them. For the time being, I created my own version of Stowe's famous novel, painting pictures in which the slave girl Alicia was able to escape from her terrible master.

The most boring were the tales of ancient Babylon, with its hanging gardens and long names that were hard to pronounce and remember. But I had no choice about what I read, and as Mama said, I was lucky to have any books at all.

When I tired of reading, Mama and I played pencil and paper games or dominoes. Sometimes I even forgot that she wasn't one of my girlfriends, we would have such fun times together.

Mama tried to be my teacher too. I didn't like math lessons, but I enjoyed English, especially when I had new vocabulary words to learn. My favorite subject was Greek mythology, with its wonderful gods and goddesses who made me forget the danger that was always around us.

Mama also taught me history, weaving tales of faraway lands and people: the Tartars, who twisted their turned-up mustaches and fought exotic battles; the Turks, with their red fezzes, and the daring Cossacks, who rode their horses so wildly, all made my imagination soar.

Sometimes Mama read some of *Pani* Olga's private books to me, the ones that were strictly forbidden by the Nazis, but I found them terribly dull. These included the biography of *Pani* Olga's hero, Lenin. Mama explained to me that he was the founder of the Communist Party and was responsible for the Russian Revolution and the overthrow of the Czar in October 1917. Lenin and two of the other Communist founders, Marx and Engels, were "like the Trinity without being holy," *Pani* Olga told *Pani* Krysia. She tried to convert her dear friend to her beliefs, but had no luck; our *Pani* was a staunch believer in Jesus Christ and *Matka Boska*.

One day *Pani* Krysia brought us two more of her friend's favorite books, *Das Kapital* by Karl Marx and the *Communist Manifesto*. Mama read them in a few days, but I thought them boring and tedious when I leafed through them. To *Pani* Olga, they were the Bible, but *Pani* Krysia was horrified that her girlfriend did not believe in God.

"But she is not stupid," she confided with a smile to Mama, "because even though she is a Communist, she at least admits that Joseph Stalin, who rules the Russians with such an iron hand, is a tyrant! Someday you'll meet her. . . . She is like a sister to me, although I can't understand her most of the time." *Pani* Krysia laughed softly. "She even tries to teach me to write. Her ideas are weird—and between you and me and the falling sky, I think she is a bit odd—but she is a true friend, and I love her dearly."

Whenever she had time, *Pani* Krysia would go upstairs to visit her friend and would usually come back looking happy. The good *Pani* Olga brought sunshine into all our lives.

One day our new friend surprised *Pani* Krysia with special gifts for me: a narrow black journal, an ink bottle of darkest ebony, and a long, thin pen. "This is for her private writing," was her message. Now when I wanted to be by myself, I could write in this diary and tell myself that I was alone no matter who else was in the room.

I would dip my pen into the magical ink and write down my thoughts and feelings in very small letters, trying to get the most out of each page. In one of my entries, I said, "I draw my pictures, and make up my little stories, which I enjoy a lot. Because when I paint I forget to be afraid, or about Papa or Janek. . . ."

Once I became involved with my writing, Mama would start to knit. She made all my skirts and sweaters from remnants of colorful wool that *Pan* Wojtek bought at the bazaar. Of course no one could even think of taking a chance to shop for me, and since I had no clothes except the dress I wore when we came to the Bajki Street apartment, I looked forward to the days when Mama finished a new garment so I could put on a different outfit.

Mama said it didn't matter that only the Wojteks would see me, or that I couldn't wear my new clothes to the park or on the street like the other children. Once the war was over, I would be all dressed up and ready to go outdoors, looking beautiful. No matter what I wore, she always made sure I had a bow in my hair, or two bows if my hair was in pigtails.

I often thought that I would be happy to go on living like this, even if I never went out, if Papa could just be with us. Outside, the Nazi storm kept sweeping through the streets. More Jews in hiding were being discovered daily; the police relied on the tip-offs of neighbors ready for a reward and used vicious dogs to search for Jews.

More than once I watched, riveted, my eyes filled with tears, as these victims were pushed roughly past our window by the armed Gestapo. Passersby on the elegant street cast curious glances at these tragic men, women, and children heading for the gates of no return.

They would never again see the blue sky or feel the rain, I thought; they would feel nothing anymore, and could no longer tell of their suffering. What would happen to them first? Would they be tortured?

When I asked Mama, she said, "Don't ask. . . . I don't know, I don't; let's not talk about it now." Already her hand would be pulling me away from the window. "Come, let's play dominoes before it gets too dark."

Some days I listened to her, but other times I would stand behind the curtained window for hours, even after the sky had darkened. Papa was out there somewhere; I strained my eyes to see him.

At night, I continued to wait for my father as I lay in bed, watching the stars. Far away beyond them was God; I trusted Him, and He protected us.

12

My happiest moment came when Papa rang the bell unexpectedly one cloudy afternoon. I threw my arms around him and started to cry while he held me tightly in his arms and covered my face with kisses. I knew how dangerous it was for him to walk on the streets, with the informers constantly on the lookout for Jews.

He told us that he almost didn't make it; he was stopped by a Ukrainian policeman. "He kept staring me in the eyes," Papa said, "and then ordered me to follow him to the police station.

" 'You goddamned Jew!' the Ukrainian said. 'What are you doing here? Where did you come from?' I began to laugh and protest that I wasn't a Jew, but the policeman didn't believe me and started to pull me over toward a doorway. He asked me for my documents and said, 'Let's go to the police station if you're so sure, Mister.' "

Papa had no Aryan papers, and he knew that he had

little hope of bluffing his way out of it, but he didn't show his fear; he had to act assured and confident. He took one hundred *złoty* out of his pocket and told the policeman that he had left his papers home in his hurry to get to an appointment, and that he would rather give the man the money. "This way," Papa had told him with a laugh, "you won't have to waste any of your time, and I can attend my meeting."

"What happened next?" I asked nervously.

"The cop looked at me for a long time. Then he shook his head and took the money—and cursing, he told me to go!" I kissed Papa and squeezed him hard. "And now I am here with you again," he said, laughing and lifting me high in the air. "Stop worrying about me. Everything will be fine." My papa, my hero, was never afraid.

He looked thin and tired, and his eyes were even sadder than before. *Pani* Wojtkowa brought him cabbage borscht and *pierogi,* which he devoured. When it grew dark, Mama, Papa, and I all climbed into "our" bed, with Papa in the middle under the covers.

It was wonderful having him right next to us. "Go to sleep," he said, kissing me on the forehead, his arms around Mama and me. The room became very quiet, peaceful, and happy. I wished so hard that he would never leave us again. "God, please make him stay," I silently prayed. "You have saved us, you are always so good to us. . . . Please protect him too."

Papa kept whispering to Mama for a long time. I heard scary words: Nazi, Gestapo, police, blackmail. He spoke of a concentration camp, Auschwitz—"a death factory constructed by the finest German scien-

101

tists, whose goal is to murder all the Jews." But it all sounded far away as I lay there, secure, next to Papa, and eventually I fell asleep.

It was still dark outside the next morning when he hugged and kissed us good-bye. He promised me that it would only be a short time now before he came back; he still hadn't found permanent hiding places for Karol and Sewer or Aunt Regina. It was getting harder and harder to find families willing to risk their lives, Papa said. "But I will work it out," he added, smiling at me. Papa was so handsome when he did not look sad.

Then he was gone again.

When I felt unhappy, when I missed my father too much, I would stand just in front of—but not too close to—the window. Looking out, I could wait for Papa and watch the children and grown-ups passing by.

Sometimes I wondered if I would ever be able to go out again, to walk and run as the kids outside did. At those times it seemed as if I would be in this room forever.

To cheer me up, Mama would suggest that I think of new picture stories and paint them. To encourage me, she would go and get my pencil and eraser out of the little cigar box where I kept them. That was all it took to get me started again, creating my sunny private world.

At other times when I was sad, Mama would try to divert me by telling me about her life before the war. Her storytelling voice was as good as a moving picture. I "met" her governess, Judith, who taught English, French, and Latin to Mama and Aunt Elsa before she left for America to become a pharmacist. She was sorry to leave the family, but she had no choice if she wanted a higher education, because in Poland, with its Jewish quota system, she could not go to a university. Mama recollected how her whole family had cried as Judith's horse-drawn carriage drove away.

My mother was proud of her education and her heritage. She told me how, when she was growing up, she'd had to learn the German language because Lwów was part of the Austrian empire. She attended first German schools, then Polish ones as Poland regained possession of the city.

Mama had also studied Hebrew, first with a tutor and then with Grandpa Henryk. She said he would have wanted me to remember one of the most important Jewish laws, the one about being a good person. "A person should always be just and honest, treating everyone the same way and helping others in need. We call this having ethics," Mama explained very seriously. "Be proud of your heritage, and follow this path in life. It would make your grandparents very happy."

After her gymnasium education, Mama married Papa. They traveled and led a busy social life, "with lots of dancing," she said. She used to meet her friends in the Café de Paris, known for the best lemonade in Lwów, or visit Grandma Fancia in her store, or go shopping with Aunt Elsa. They were not only sisters, Mama told me; they were best friends.

My beautiful, dark-haired, blue-eyed aunt Elsa was only sixteen years old when she ran away and got married to Uncle Leon. He was a very learned man, a gymnasium professor; Aunt Elsa met him when she won the school beauty contest. Grandma Fancia and Grandpa Henryk were very angry with Aunt Elsa when she ran away, but then they made up with her.

Mama and I would also talk about our happy times together, which I didn't remember very well. Those were the days when fear had no place in our lives. Now danger was around us all the time, from the big placards that were posted on the street buildings, encouraging people to turn in the Jews, to the many neighbors and even friends who were suddenly for hire by the Gestapo.

Pan Wojtek kept telling Mama to cheer up, that the war would be over soon. The Americans were helping the Russians to win, he said, and the rumor was that Mr. Roosevelt, the American president, would be sure to save all the Jews. Then everything would be normal again, and he would be the landlord of this building— "a gift from his grateful friends, the *Pan* and *Pani* Landau." In the meantime, the weeks passed slowly.

Early one Sunday morning, we heard a sudden, firm knock on the door. We jumped up, and Mama and I climbed quickly into our hiding place.

Pani Krysia snatched the sheets from her sofa and threw them into the closet so that anyone who might enter the bedroom would see only the two unmade beds. Then she put on her robe and rushed to the door.

A few minutes later, we heard footsteps in the bedroom approaching our window. Mama squeezed my hand. "It's me, it is safe," we heard *Pani* Krysia say. She lifted the rug and opened our trapdoor. There, in the middle of the room, stood Sewer.

My cousin was still handsome, even though almost all his blond, wavy hair had been cut off. He was full of hugs and kisses, and he smiled as he tried to kid with me. But he spent only a short time with us and would not tell me where he and Karol were staying. It was better that I should not know, he said. But when he came back again, he added, he would let me know for sure.

Then it was time for him to go. Sewer told me to stop crying and kissed me good-bye. I watched him through the window as he quickly crossed the street and turned the corner, his head down.

When I looked back at Mama, I saw that her face was wet. I sat down on the couch next to her and put my arms around her; then I took her hand in mine and started to wipe her tears away. A church bell rang, nine times, and I remember thinking: Will the war ever end? Will we ever get out of here?

Winter came; the streets were covered with snow and the windows were often sheets of ice, with only small openings to look through. One wintry afternoon, when we decided to clean up the closet in the bedroom, danger knocked on our door again.

It was really my fault, because I did not want to read or play or paint anymore that day. I was just as angry and miserable as the windy weather outside. Then Mama suggested that we do something different: We would surprise *Pani* Krysia by cleaning up the metal wardrobe.

We had finished taking all the Wojteks' clothes from the closet shelves and putting them on the sofa and over the beds when there was a sudden, hard knock on the front door. Mama and I froze. *Pani* Krysia swiftly locked our bedroom door, and almost immediately the police were in the kitchen.

We had been sitting on the floor, separating *Pani* Krysia's beads and buttons. Mama grabbed my hand and squeezed it hard. I dropped the rosary beads I had been holding into my lap; my heart was beating so loud that I worried they might hear it. I did not dare to move.

In the kitchen, we could hear an angry man ordering *Pani* Krysia to let him into the bedroom. Then someone tried to open the locked door. I watched, frozen, as the knob turned.

The Ukrainian policeman commanded *Pani* Wojtkowa to find the key and open the door right away. No reason was given. Did they already know about us, or did they want the apartment for their own *Volksdeutche?*

Mama held me tight as I stared at the door. They could break it down at any minute; I could picture a strong, uniformed man with a cruel face pushing at the door. Tears started to roll down my cheeks as I heard *Pani* Krysia explaining that she couldn't find the key. They shouted and cursed at her in anger.

Did *Pani* Krysia think we could make it to our secret window? I looked up at Mama, but she shook her head and then pointed to the pants, underwear, and socks spread all over the room. It looked as if someone had been right in the middle of cleaning out the closet and had had to leave suddenly. Even if we made it to the window, they would be sure to come back with their dogs and sniff us out right away.

I heard *Pani* Krysia say that she had to keep the door

locked because of all the robberies in the area. Her husband usually carried the key with him, she said; could they come back tomorrow, maybe?

The angry policeman told her that if she did not find the key in the next couple of minutes, they would break down the door. We could hear *Pani* Krysia's heavy footsteps on the kitchen floor as she continued to walk slowly to different cabinets, pretending to look for the key.

I was numb. Our lives were coming to an end. They would come and take us away . . . forever.

And then Mama made a decision. She got up slowly from the floor and pulled me up with her. Very quietly, on tiptoes, we slid to the other end of the room, trying not to make the wooden floor squeak. Mama moved the rug aside and opened the trapdoor. Then she pushed me up, and I climbed inside the secret window. She followed, and we pulled the little trapdoor shut again.

I was standing on the windowsill, next to my diary and my watercolors. "Please, God, make the rug stop moving before they break into the room," I prayed. If they suspected anything, they would come back with dogs. . . . I could almost hear them barking.

If they took us, I thought, our possessions would be destroyed also. No one would ever know about my precious writing and my paintings. . . .

Mama held me tight, her arms wrapped around me. The windowsill was narrow but large enough for us to stand sideways. Mama whispered in my ear that everything would be all right, but my tears did not want to listen. They kept pouring down my face.

Then we heard footsteps approaching our hiding place.

I buried my head in Mama's arms and closed my eyes, thinking, This is the end.

Someone was lifting the rug and opening our trap-door. It was *Pani* Krysia. "They are gone," she said, smiling and sighing at the same time as she reached for me.

I couldn't stop crying and shaking. The police had left; *Pani* Krysia had convinced them that she did not have the key. If they wanted to see the bedroom, she had said, they would have to come back after her husband returned from the market. *He* had the key.

Pani Krysia had decided that it was too dangerous to let them in with all the clothes spread around the room. She was happy to have made the right decision.

After that, we were even more careful than before; I knew that we could never clean up the closet again. For the next few weeks, I stopped using my watercolors and only drew with my pencil, while Mama didn't knit at all. We read a lot, ready to climb into our secret window at the slightest possibility of danger without leaving a trace behind us.

Filled with fear, we waited and waited, but the police never came back to look at the apartment. God was truly watching over us.

13

T OWARD THE MIDDLE OF DECEMBER 1943, I became very sick with scarlet fever. Since of course I couldn't see a doctor, Mama had to use a medical book to nurse me. I remember that I had a wet rag on my forehead the whole time and liked the feeling of coolness over my eyes.

During my illness I had a terrible dream about hospitals and an old, mean doctor who tied my hands behind my back. Perhaps these were buried memories from before the war, when I traveled by train to Vienna with Mama and our governess to have my tonsils out. We stayed with Mama's Viennese relatives who— I still remember—bought me a toy that was in the height of fashion at that time, a boy windup doll that moved with great speed. Mama later told me that while I was in the hospital, I kept biting the renowned hand of my doctor. This very famous professor was a Jew who would later operate on Hitler and was eventually allowed to leave Vienna for London.

I had a very painful sore throat and high temperature with my scarlet fever, and I still had not learned to be a good patient. When I suddenly awoke from a nap one afternoon and jumped up with a loud scream, Mama jammed her fist into my mouth with so much strength that she knocked out my back tooth.

I fell back on the bed, crying. My mouth began to bleed, and I was so full of pain and anger that I screamed again without any thought to who might hear me. I remember thinking, Let her knock another tooth out! as I challenged my mother with a defiant look.

But Mama only looked at me for what seemed a very long minute and said nothing. Afterward, I was mad at myself and started to worry that somebody would call the police. No one did; *Pan* Wojtek told Mama that the ears of the walls were probably all plugged up with the snow that had fallen that day.

It was Christmastime; outside the bedroom windows, elegantly decorated horses pulled black lacquered sleds with passengers wrapped up in cozy plaid blankets. Sometimes a car sped by. Children, bundled in colorful hats and scarves, threw snowballs at each other with mittened hands. Ladies in beautiful fur coats smiled as they strolled by, linked arm in arm with uniformed German officers. I could see them all from behind the curtained window, could imagine the sound of their polished boots trampling the pure white snow.

Christmas day came, but the Wojteks did not buy a tree. *Pan* Wojtek explained to me that since he had no family or friends, there was no point in having one. Instead, his wife bought a big ham and made a special Christmas dinner with *gołąbki* (stuffed cabbage), *pierogi, paluszki* ("fingers" of boiled dough), and other delicacies that even her husband liked.

For many people, it was a day to celebrate with family. I kept looking for Papa, whom we hadn't seen for many months. When I asked Mama about him, she said, "I know he must be somewhere, *kochanie,* but I can't tell you where."

"Do *you* know where he is?" I asked, confused.

She said she didn't. "It's better this way," she kept repeating.

I didn't understand. Was it better because if we were discovered and made to talk, we really wouldn't know? Mama wouldn't explain. She said *Pan* Wojtek was in touch with Papa from time to time, and that he was fine; I had to be satisfied with that.

The sleighbells jingled in the distance, but they did not bring my papa.

In January 1944, on Mama's birthday, I gave her a present I had made—a card with a bunch of red flowers and a poem. Mama was touched; I had painted the picture in secret, covering it with my hand, and surprised her. She kissed me and held me tight, and I could feel her swallowing her tears, not wanting me to see them. She said it was the prettiest pot of flowers she had ever seen.

On a gray, snowy afternoon, our bedroom door suddenly swung open and *Pan* Wojtek angrily stormed in, carrying a wooden cane and wearing four hats on top of his head. He looked ridiculous! Mama and I were in the middle of a domino game, but we stopped quickly when we saw him.

His face red from excitement, he rushed toward

Mama and grabbed her hand. "Listen, my *Pani,* to what happened to me today!" He pulled a chair to the table, facing us, and sat down with all his hats on.

I kept digging my upper lip over my lower one, trying very hard not to laugh, as I listened to his story. I knew better than to anger him.

"As I was walking toward the bazaar to sell your husband's watch, I saw a big crowd standing around an old man who was selling men's hats. When I saw all these people, I quickly ran to him before he could sell them out, but since nobody was buying, the man dropped his prices in half, and I knew right away that I had a bargain!

"I bought all four hats, and instead of carrying them, I put them on top of my head. It was easier that way, you know, and much warmer. Then I started for home. On the way I picked up this cane"—he pointed to the beat-up wooden stick—"and I was happy with my terrific bargains until—" Now he stopped and cursed. "*Psiakrew!* (Damn it!) Until some boys, some damned snotnoses saw me!"

I could just imagine *Pan* Wojtek walking down the street with four hats on his head and being spotted by a group of boys. I wished I had been there with them!

"This gang, may they never see light again, started to call me names and laugh at me. Imagine calling me a 'crazy hat man,' a 'lunatic'! They stuck out their tongues, and before I knew it, they started throwing stones at me! At me, *Pan* Michaj Wojtek! I was ready to choke them to death with my bare hands, believe me, my *Pani,* I was all ready! But they ran faster than I . . . I could not catch them. . . . But wait! I am not finished!"

Pan Wojtek's voice was getting louder and louder, and his face was twisted with fury. "Terrible, terrible," Mama murmured, looking very serious. Then she got up and told him she was going to get him a drink of water from the kitchen.

From the corner of my eye I could see him watching me angrily. Could he read my mind? I did not look up. He continued sitting there with his four hats on.

After he had sipped his water, he moved his chair closer to Mama and began to whisper to her about how he would get his revenge on the boys. "I will sneak up on them at night and catch them with my hatchet, and then I will chop the head off each one of them! It's not hard, not at all. Remember, I am not a coward, *Pani*. Just wait and see!"

I could hear him clearly despite his attempt to whisper. He's a madman, I thought.

Mama put her hand on his shoulder. "That is a dangerous plan, *Pan* Michaj," she said quietly. "If you kill them, the Gestapo will find you out and come to the apartment right away! They will take us all away and kill us. . . . You don't want that to happen. No, the best way is to wait until after the war. Then you can get even with them . . . I guarantee you, it's better that way."

Suddenly, I just couldn't hold back my laughter any longer. It was out before I even knew it.

For a split second, he stared at me in shock. Then he exploded with anger as he jumped toward me. Mama moved quickly in front of him, and I hid behind her, trembling.

"I'll kill you, little miss!" he shouted. "I'll kill you! Go to the streets, let's see how smart you'll be when the Gestapo gets you! You— You—" He turned to Mama and screamed, "I want her out! Out!!"

Terrified, I began to cry. *Pan* Wojtek stopped yelling and began wiping his face with a handkerchief as Mama begged him to let me stay. She nudged me and I apologized.

He looked at me, cursed me, and walked out of the bedroom to the kitchen. We stayed in the apartment, and I promised Mama I would never laugh at him again, but she was furious with me. I knew he had meant every word; he wanted to throw me out. He hated me!

For the next few days, I didn't dare to look at *Pan* Wojtek, I was so scared of him. Then one day, during a domino game, Mama noticed that I was looking very worried.

"What's the matter?" she asked.

Suddenly all the tears I had been holding back poured out. I told her about the fear that had been growing inside me ever since the incident with *Pan* Wojtek.

"What will happen to us," I finally asked Mama, "if Germany wins the war? Will we have to stay here forever with crazy *Pan* Michaj, who despises me?"

Mama wrapped her arms around me. "The war will be over soon, silly! Don't you worry—the Russians and the Americans are going to win. The Red Army will come and liberate us; we will *not* stay with the Wojteks forever!"

I felt immensely relieved. We both laughed and began another game of dominoes.

I decided to write a silly rhyming poem about nutty

Pan Wojtek in my diary. On paper, I could say all the things about him that I couldn't say in real life, and nobody could stop me—nobody! I didn't have to like him, even though he let me stay . . . stay, and wait for our liberation.

One rainy afternoon, we were in the kitchen whispering with *Pani* Krysia when we heard a knock on the front door. Mama quickly grabbed her knitting, but as we ran to the bedroom, she dropped her spool of red wool on the kitchen floor and forgot to let go of the end of the thread. *Pani* Krysia locked the door and then, as always, hid the key in the drawer before opening the front door. A neighbor, *Pani* Zozkolnikowa, came in.

Even though we could hear the woman talking to *Pani* Krysia, Mama began to pull her end of the wool thread without thinking and the spool started rolling across the kitchen floor toward our bedroom door. I heard the neighbor innocently ask, "My dear *Pani*, whom do you hide in there?"

I quickly ripped the end of the thread. On the other side of the door, *Pani* Krysia was laughing as she tried to explain that the window was open in the bedroom and the wind had "probably blown the wool across the floor."

Then *Pani* Zozkolnikowa pulled the loose end of the thread, and I saw it disappear under the little space between the door and the floor. I glanced at Mama's white face and quivering lips. We stood there, petrified, our lives suspended in that narrow space.

She stayed and talked with *Pani* Krysia for a while

longer and then left. For the next few days we spent a lot of time in our window, feeling helpless. She had to have known that somebody was in the bedroom. Would she sell her soul, like Faust in Goethe's book that *Pani* Olga had brought to us? The Gestapo paid its informers well.

Two weeks went by but the police did not come. *Pani* Zozkolnikowa decided not to report us.

Time seemed to be playing tricks, moving very slowly when I wanted it to leap forward. Would the Russians ever come to rescue us, or would we die in this apartment?

Pan Wojtek continued to beat his wife and call her insulting names, even though he had promised Mama he would stop. *Pani* Krysia still tried to climb on the window ledge when he went after her; now she threatened not only to scream for the Gestapo but to tell them that he had forced her to hide "the Jewish woman and her child." We knew that she did not mean it, but it was still very frightening and dangerous. We had to run to our secret hiding place each time this happened, just in case the police really did come storming in.

14

THE ICE ON OUR WINDOWS began to melt, and slush covered the street below. Slowly the leaves on the trees in front of our building began to appear, and we still did not hear anything from Papa. I kept asking Mama about him.

She was vague and hesitant. She said that she didn't really know where he was; he was no longer at the last hiding place. When I asked if he had escaped into the woods, she said that she didn't know. "Maybe he is somewhere else. . . . We just have to wait."

"You always say that!" I told her angrily.

"What else is there to do?" she asked me.

In those bottomless, dreadful hours, I kept standing by the window stubbornly, hoping to see Papa on the street. Then slowly, cracks of doubt began to form in my mind, followed by a frightening thought: What if . . . ?

I could not, did not want to think about it. What

would we do without Papa? Once we left the Wojteks' apartment, where would we go?

As always, Mama told me not to worry. Papa would probably come back, and if not . . . "It will all work out," she said, but I didn't know how.

"It would be very dangerous for you to live alone after liberation, because there are still a lot of people who hate the Jews," *Pani* Krysia told Mama one night, thinking I was sleeping. "Maybe you could go to Palestine if *Pan* Landau does not come back?"

"I don't know . . . maybe he will return. Maybe he just can't reach us, maybe it's too risky—who knows?" Mama answered, as I held my breath so they would not hear me.

Doubt and hope battled within me, the doubt slowly stealing my hope away. I cried to myself when Mama was asleep.

One afternoon an air-raid siren suddenly pierced the air, signaling the approach of Soviet planes in the skies of Lwów. We heard the panicked screams of people on the street and the cries of children as everyone rushed inside. Their feet pounded the stairs as they hurried down to the cellar. I stood behind the curtain, watching, until Mama pulled me toward the windowless bathroom, our shelter. It was safer for us than the bedroom because our room faced the building across the street that was occupied by the Gestapo. It seemed as if the Soviet bombs were aimed there.

She sat on the edge of the tub and hugged me close to her. Sitting in the blackness of the little room, waiting for the air raid to stop, I kept thinking of Papa. Maybe he was somewhere with Sewer and Karol now, hiding from the bombs just as we were. But my uncertainty would always return.

What would we do without Papa after the war?

We had property in Lwów; maybe we could move to one of our own apartment buildings? At least we would get back Mama's fur coat, and the silver fox with its beautiful long tail that Papa had given to her for her birthday. We had left these things, and the merchandise from Grandma Fancia's store, with various Christian friends right before the Russians entered our city in 1939.

Grandma Fancia had closed up her store just in time, before the Red Army could take everything away. It had been a big task to pack the whole store up in boxes; all the staff was gone by then. Mama and Papa and even I had helped out.

My grandmother had put all the ladies' garments and rolls of fabric into big brown boxes: elegant slips, nightgowns, silky pajamas, stockings with black seams, underwear, and fancy panties with lace trimming. My mother had helped her to fit everything together as tightly as possible.

I had loved helping Grandma on that day. I remember how she stroked my black pigtails as I busily sorted buttons, thread, snaps, hooks, and multicolored ribbons. She had softly spoken her thoughts aloud: "The clothing may survive this war, but I don't think I will ever see it again."

She had been right. The rolls of fabric, nightgowns, and lingerie still existed, but my beautiful, loving grandmother was only a memory.

The air raids continued to come and go. Some were just false alarms. They were a good sign, Mama told me; the Russians were getting closer and the war would be over soon. I knew I should be happy, not scared, but still I prayed that we would stay alive through the bombing and make it to the end.

In the middle of one moonlit night in May, an air raid left several buildings across the street in flames. A siren announced that the danger was over, and Mama and I had just crawled back into our beds when the kitchen door burst open. The Wojteks had returned from the cellar with a couple of Polish neighbors who were eager to watch the fire from our bedroom. They said our window offered the best view of the bombed buildings; I could hear them in the kitchen, talking excitedly.

It happened so fast that we didn't have time to get into our secret hiding place. In a split second, *Pani* Krysia left everyone in front of the kitchen window, ran into our bedroom, and threw her sheets and pillows onto our bed, motioning to us to hide. At that moment, Mama pushed me into the darkest corner of the room, behind the tall ceramic stove, and pressed herself against the only wall that was in the shadows. The light from the flames across the street lit the rest of the room; I could only pray that no one would spot us.

Pani Krysia immediately rejoined her neighbors, and a couple of minutes later they entered the bedroom, almost touching my nightgown as they surged past me toward the two front windows. Though they talked loudly, all speaking at the same time as they watched the burning building, I could not understand their words; all I could hear was the pounding of my own heart. I held my breath, unable to swallow, trying to flatten myself against the cold tiles of the stove.

They were laughing and joking around, their faces pressed to the glass. I watched them from my corner in the darkness. Would they ever leave? If only my heart would stop making so much noise!

Their words slowly started to take on meaning. . . . Now I could hear *Pan* Wojtek discussing the Germans' fear of the Russians; I knew from his voice that he was very nervous, but his wife spoke naturally. It was not until they had finally left and I ran into Mama's arms that *Pani* Krysia covered her face and began to cry.

Did they see us? Would they report us to the Gestapo? That night hardly anyone could fall asleep. I could hear the turning and twisting, the creaking springs.

"What will happen to us all now?" asked *Pani* Krysia the next morning. Mama tried to reassure her that they did not see us—but did she really believe this, or was she just saying it?

Pan Wojtek did not go to the bazaar that day. Everyone was on edge, hoping, waiting, and hoping again that no one had seen us. The day passed quietly, followed by the next one. Another week went by without further incident. *Pan* Michaj returned to the bazaar; Staś was knocking on the door at his usual time. They did not come to get us.

In June 1944, in the middle of the night, another heavy bombing took place. The sound of the sirens tore the air; bells attached to each building for this purpose began to gong.

We could hear the frightened tenants in the building

shouting, "Everybody up! They're bombing! Hurry! Quick!" And as the Wojteks fled to the cellar along with the rest of the people, Mama and I rushed to the bathroom. After the raid was over, the Wojteks told us that many people had been killed this time.

Early the next morning, when we heard another siren, we ran to the kitchen after the Wojteks left for the cellar. I was heading for the bathroom when suddenly I heard Mama cry out. A grenade had pierced the kitchen window, and part of it had lodged itself in her foot. Before I could utter a word, she reached down and pulled a piece of metal out of a hole above her left ankle.

I stood staring, unable to move, but she pulled me along as the blood flowed out onto the linoleum. "Hurry!" she cried, and we continued our flight to the bathroom. Frantically I grabbed a towel and wrapped it around her leg, but I couldn't stop the bleeding.

When the sirens finally signaled that the raid was over, the Wojteks entered the kitchen and locked the door. *Pani* Krysia saw the blood and screamed, then flew to the bathroom and began washing Mama's foot right away. I watched her as I held Mama's hand. How gentle and tender she was! Tears covered my mother's face, but she did not complain.

I couldn't stop crying. "It's all my fault, I should have run faster," I sobbed while *Pani* Krysia bandaged the wound. Mama's face was white and her hands were trembling, but she tried to smile.

Pan Wojtek had been silently staring at Mama, almost in shock, but suddenly he exploded. "It's all because of you!" he shouted at me, his eyes filled with

Friends Playing Dominoes · In the long months of hiding, my mother became my girlfriend and teacher. We played many domino games together.

Master Beating Alicia the Slave Girl · I painted a series of pictures about the slave Alicia's experiences after reading *Uncle Tom's Cabin*. Although at that time in Poland I had never seen black people, I identified with their suffering.

Finding a Kind Lady to Hide Alicia Was Not Easy · We were just fortunate to have found Christians willing to risk their lives to hide Mama and me.

Maryla Is Visited by the Doctor · This and the next painting are from the booklet I called "Doctor Series." The little girl in the picture has scarlet fever; friends and a doctor come to see her. When I had this illness, my mother used a medical book to nurse me.

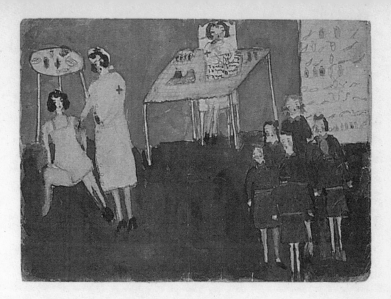

Vaccination in School · The only memory I had of a needle was the operation on my tonsils in Austria before the war.

Long Live Mama · In January 1944 I made this birthday card for my mother, the only gift I could give her.

Eva's Sweater Business · I painted a series of pictures about this girl, based on the incident with wool that almost cost us our lives.

She Sells All Her Sweaters · Though the girl Eva knit sweaters in my story, it was Mama who hand-knit all my clothes.

The Sea Adventure—Escape · I had never actually seen an ocean but envisioned it according to what I had read in Jules Verne's adventures. Escape was always on our minds.

A Summer Home in the Country · Painted after reading Tolstoi and perhaps from stories Mama told me about her childhood vacations with her parents. I wished that one day we too could visit such a beautiful home in the country.

Kindergarten Class · This watercolor and the next one are from the booklet I called "Growing Up From Kindergarten On." I wished that I too could walk outdoors like the children I watched from behind our window.

On the Way to the Gymnasium · I hoped that, like Mama, I would be allowed to go to a gymnasium one day.

Girl Brushing Dog in Bath · This picture and the next are from the booklet I called "Dog Is My Friend." In reality I was terrified of dogs, since the Germans used them to hunt Jews.

Girl With a Dog · This shows the fence and garden of the Bajki Street apartment building.

After a Full Day a Bath Is Prepared by a Chambermaid · In reality my mother and I hid in the bathroom during air raids while everyone else ran to the cellar.

Liberation · I painted this representation of a goddess of freedom just before the Red Army arrived in 1944.

hate. He angrily pointed his finger at me, almost touching my face, and I looked away, scared.

Mama spoke up, looking straight at him. "It was no one's fault, *Pan* Wojtek. No one's! You can't blame the child!" He listened, still staring furiously at me, then walked out of the bathroom and slammed the bedroom door behind him. For the next few days, Mama could hardly walk, but then *Pan* Wojtek bought her a cane and she moved around more easily.

Of all the air raids that followed, one that came late on a Sunday evening in June almost sealed our fate. First came a heavy raid; then, before the siren announced that the danger had officially passed, *Pan* Wojtek returned from the cellar, sat down in the kitchen near the window, and lit a cigarette. Mama and I went back to the bedroom with *Pani* Krysia.

Almost immediately we heard a terrible banging on the front door, with shouts ordering us to open up. We could hear furious German voices in the corridor, and Mama and I quickly climbed into the window. *Pani* Krysia threw her sheets into the closet, cleared the sofa of all evidence that she had slept there, and then rushed to the front door.

Pan Wojtek spoke Polish to the police, and they yelled back in German, but Mama and I couldn't hear their words. What had he done to make them so angry?

We heard *Pani* Wojtkowa sobbing loudly, and then suddenly the door slammed. It was quiet—too quiet. What could have brought the Germans into the apartment? Were they looking for us? Mama tried to comfort me; I could not stop crying. I knew that they would come and get us now; they would torture us first, and then kill us. . . .

After an eternity of waiting, footsteps softly approached our secret window, and I stopped breathing as the rug was lifted and the trapdoor opened. I closed my eyes . . . this was the end . . . but instead, there was *Pani* Krysia in tears, wringing her hands.

As we descended into the room, she kept repeating that it was all her husband's fault. "He should have known better; he never should have started to smoke before the alarm was called off. Such a stupid idiot!"

She explained that when the Germans saw the light of *Pan* Wojtek's cigarette through the kitchen window, they thought he was giving signals to the Russian planes. Now they had taken him away. "Jesus . . . Maria, Mother of God . . . what will happen next? If they think he is a spy, they will come back to search us. . . . *Boże mój!* (My God!) They will find you, *Pani* Landau!" Mama placed her hands over her face.

"*Boże mój!* What now?" cried *Pani* Krysia frantically, walking around the room. She suddenly stopped in front of Mama and stared at us. "You must go! You must! There is no place where I can hide you!" She continued pacing back and forth, invoking the help of the Holy Mother Maria.

"Please, please, *Pani* Wojtkowa, we can't leave; we can't," Mama begged, following her and trying to persuade her to let us stay.

"You must!" *Pani* Wojtkowa demanded.

"We have no place to go," Mama tearfully said. "We must stay in here, *Pani* Krysia. Please understand. . . ."

I cried and urged Mama to leave before the Germans

returned. All we had to do was unlock the iron fence, get into the street, and keep on walking toward the woods at the outskirts of town. Then we could join the partisans. But if we waited, the Gestapo would come to get us!

Mama refused even to discuss leaving. I didn't realize the danger, she said; the Gestapo or a passerby would pick us up if we put one foot outside. "We would not last five minutes," she told me. "No, we must stay. The Germans will not come back. They will believe *Pan* Wojtek's story; they will be able to tell that he is not a spy."

Pani Krysia was still trembling, but Mama finally convinced her that we should stay. We had no choice.

In the end, we crawled back into our secret window and waited for what seemed thousands of hours. I held on to Mama, who whispered to me about the wonderful things we would do once the Russians came, when everything would be fine again. We waited, and waited, and waited; I needed to use the bathroom but knew that I couldn't go.

And then at last *Pan* Wojtek came home. Looking exhausted, he told us that the Gestapo had pricked his legs with pins "to see if he had any reflexes." When he told them that he didn't feel anything, they had slapped his face, called him a dumb Pole, cursed him, and made him pay a fine. They made him promise never to smoke in front of the window again, or else they would shoot him next time. Then they let him go. He had to walk for hours to get home.

I had never seen him so shaken. He was still trembling all over as he told Mama how careful he would be in the future. "I will never dare to use the lighter in front of the window again. No, no, my *Pani*. . . ."

Again we were spared; again, God was good.

From behind the curtained window I watched as summer splashed sunshine over Bajki Street. The children had discarded their scarves and jackets; shoes had replaced boots, and a balloon drifted past our window, so close I could almost touch it. Yet the Nazis were still here, still part of the street scene as they strolled by. "Germany is now like a wounded dog," said *Pan* Wojtek, "who cannot live any longer, but keeps fighting to the last drop of blood."

I hoped he was right. In the meantime, the Russians kept attacking, and I wondered if we would survive or be killed by bombs. Most of the air raids took place at night, but sometimes the planes surprised us during the day. Everybody else in our building continued to run to the cellar, while Mama hobbled with me to the bathroom.

The whole house trembled with the thunder of the bombs, but the hinges miraculously stayed on the bathroom door. Mama held onto it, trying to keep it closed in case *Pani* Krysia should walk in with a neighbor, as she sat on the edge of the tub and hugged me tight. I was getting used to the air raids and wasn't so afraid of them now.

The Germans continued to walk below our window. The air was filled with the glow of summer; I could smell it when the window was slightly open. But the sun did not touch the inside of our room; I could only watch the summer days from behind my window, and paint women and children enjoying their freedom outdoors. Rain or shine, I continued to look for Papa, waiting for that big surprise when I would see him cross the street.

Sometimes *Pan* Wojtek brought the newspaper home. "They only print lies," he said. "Why bother to look at it?" But Mama still liked to see the paper, even if it was only propaganda, and sometimes she told the news to *Pan* Michaj and *Pani* Krysia, because neither of them could read. She could get around better now; she walked much more slowly, but we were thankful that no infection had set in from her wound.

Some Poles listened to secret radios, and *Pan* Wojtek came home from the bazaar with many different rumors. The Russian troops were approaching. . . . The Germans were losing, "nearly finished," and they were more afraid of the Russians than they were of the Americans. But despite these assurances we saw no changes around us. The German officers still paraded by with their polished boots and confident looks.

One afternoon, *Pani* Krysia came home with terrible news. On our kitchen door, the words "Jews are hidden here" had been scribbled in white chalk. *Pani* Krysia had wiped the door off quickly, but she was scared. "Someone in this building knows you are here," she said, shaking all over.

She continued to talk nervously, all out of breath. "It had to be someone who was too afraid to go to the police, yet wanted someone else to find out and report us. Who could it be?" she asked herself, as if we were not even there. "Who?"

"What should we do now?" I asked Mama frantically. "Should we run away?"

"No," Mama answered. "We must stay; there's no

place for us to go." This time *Pani* Krysia agreed; and so we stayed. Days came and went. . . . The police did not come.

A couple of days after *Pani* Krysia found the chalk writing on the door, three Jews passed below our window, their heads bent as they were pushed along by Gestapo wielding rubber truncheons. A girl and a small boy, holding a woman's hands. For them, it was over. They had been discovered hiding in a building just across the street, denounced by a Pole, *Pan* Wojtek told us the next day.

I couldn't stop picturing those children's faces as I continued to look out the window, searching the crowded street for Papa. What if he never returned to us?

Time continued to pass slowly on those endlessly long, warm days. Mama carefully reread the newspaper, checking the narrow columns for clues, trying to dig out some truth from under the piles of words; it was like a puzzle, she said, spending hours gazing at various articles in her constant quest for some good news. We went on waiting for the Red Army to liberate us and wondering if they would ever come.

15

AND THEN, on a beautiful day in July 1944, the Soviet Army finally entered Lwów.

Pani Krysia came hurrying in, so excited she could hardly speak. The Germans were running away; it was really happening!

All of us stood behind the curtained window and watched the Germans dropping little bundles behind them, pushing and cursing in their haste to get away from the approaching Russians. A lost child was crying; a man with a camera grabbed the little boy and pulled him into a building, then went out again and started to take pictures of the running soldiers.

The street was in panic, with people scurrying in different directions. A skinny young soldier was stripping off his officer's jacket and throwing it to the street. He angrily shouted, *"Wir werden zurückkommen!* (We will return!)" as he ran.

"The cursed Germans are paying the highest prices

for civilian clothes," *Pan* Wojtek said, smiling, as he joined us at the window. "They will give you anything for a pair of old pants, a caftan, or a coat—watches, gold, rings, and diamonds! The Lucifers, may they croak before I give them anything! Barbarians!"

A few young women attached themselves to the soldiers, pulling their babies behind them; some ran after the men with baby carriages.

"God curse the collaborators; let them burn in hell! Let them burn!" And *Pan* Wojtek spat contemptuously on the floor. "Wait till the Ruski soldiers get them! Oh, will they dance, these 'choleras' with their babies!"

I squeezed Mama's hand. The last German had disappeared. Shooting could be heard in the distance. Then someone shouted, "The Germans are gone!" I saw heavy trucks approaching and opened the window.

"Wait, wait, you must not be so careless," Mama warned me, but I didn't want to listen; I ran out into the street. It was flooded with Russian tanks full of dusty soldiers waving their caps, laughing, and hollering, "*Zdravstvuite!* (Hello!)" The joy of that moment is forever engraved in my memory.

I inhaled the fresh air, breathing deeply. Oh, to be free—to no longer be afraid! Where to look first?

Mama was right behind me. From one end to the other, Russian soldiers filled the street. The blend of noises was like a celebration of life itself—voices singing, trucks rumbling, somewhere a harmonica playing a Soviet song. A building was burning across the street, encircled in orange and purple flames.

A young soldier with a red star on his cap smiled

and waved at me, and I pushed away Mama's hand and ran toward his truck. He bent down and picked me up in his arms, lifting me high in the sky.

The truck was not moving, so I climbed in next to him. A woman soldier decorated with Stalin and Lenin medals threw me a piece of candy from another truck, and I caught it and waved back to her. *"Spasibo!* (Thank you!)" I called out.

Mama still had a worried look on her face. She stood close to me, talking with a soldier who tried to convince her that the Russians were really going to stay in Lwów—that the Germans would never return. "For sure?" she asked again.

Suddenly a tremendous explosion shook the air, and the street was covered with shattered glass.

"The Germans are blowing up a building!" someone shouted. Mama frantically grabbed me and pulled me down from the truck, and we started to run toward the apartment building. Despite the explosions, I was not scared; it felt so good to be outside! We entered our corridor, and once I was inside, I opened the windows wide and let the curtains blow softly in the wind.

At Mama's insistence we stayed in that evening. When I awoke the next morning, the window was open, the sun was shining, and I could hear the loud, happy voices of the Russians, mixed with laughter and singing. I pushed the curtain aside, and for the first time I stuck my head out and looked down at the street below me without being afraid. It wasn't a dream—we were free, and I could go outside again.

The Red Army stayed in Lwów. Only the Polish neighbors were left in our building; our secret was a piece of news whispered from one tenant to another, until they all knew that the Wojteks had hidden two Jews. Some found this incredible; others said they had suspected it all along.

In the days that followed the liberation, I tried to hold onto my belief that we would see Papa again. Maybe he had been one of the lucky ones; after all, there were still miracles—but reality slowly ground away at my dreams.

Pan Wojtek told Mama that he had heard of a place where Jewish survivors were gathering, and one afternoon we set out toward the address that *Pan* Michaj had given us, filled with hope.

There were hardly any civilians on the street; only masses of Russian soldiers, trucks, and tanks painted with the red hammer-and-sickle symbol. We passed bombed buildings, wrecked automobiles, loose telephone wires, broken glass, and pieces of grenade shells; some areas were cordoned off with signs in Russian and Polish warning of the dangers of an explosion.

After we had walked for some time, Mama grew tired, leaning heavily on her cane, and we slowed down. She and I had been worrying about what would happen to us if the Germans returned. We could never go back to the Wojteks; all the neighbors knew about us by now. What would we do?

I asked Mama, who agreed that it would be catastrophic. "We must follow the Red Army toward the East if that should happen," she said. "We must . . . if they would take us."

Her leg began to throb after we had been walking

for about an hour, and we sat down on the doorstep of an empty, demolished building. I felt hot and tired too. Two officers, their chests covered with medals, approached us; they wanted to know where we were heading.

"Nowhere, now," Mama answered. Still remembering her Russian, she asked if—should the Germans come back—we could possibly join them.

One of the officers laughed. "The German dogs are beaten already; you have nothing to worry about!" he assured her. Then he paused and looked very serious. "It would be impossible for us to take you along, but don't be afraid, comrade. They are finished, kaput, forever; they will never come back!" He wiped his sweaty forehead and walked toward a truck filled with soldiers; the other officer was already signaling to him to hurry up.

"Do svidania! (Good-bye!)" they called out. "Don't be afraid!" and the military caravan moved on, sending the street dust flying behind them. I waved, and they waved back.

We continued to walk. Suddenly from a side street emerged a hunched man holding a small boy's hand. The child's dark, sunken eyes held a look that frightened me; he was probably five or six years old.

Silently they fell in step with us. After a few minutes, I asked the boy's name, but he just kept on walking and looking down without answering me. Then his father told me that Szrulek could not speak.

"He lost his voice during one of the most vicious 'actions' . . . but I will go to the best doctors! The best!" He turned to Mama and explained that Szrulek had seen his mother and baby sister beaten terribly by the Gestapo and then shot. He had been hiding behind a jar of pickles in a cellar. Afterward, he could not utter a single word; he had lost his voice.

I took the candy that the woman officer had given me from my pocket and squeezed it into Szrulek's hand; he looked up and smiled at me. His father was telling Mama that an old Ukrainian grave digger had hidden them in a grave in a cemetery for almost a year. He had brought them food and drink and, in the winter, a blanket, coming mostly on moonless and starless nights. Luckily, he was never caught. This was their first trip out; his legs felt tired and stiff, he said, from the months of lying curled up like a pretzel.

Like Mama, he had heard about a meeting place where the few remaining Jews gathered in hope of finding their relatives, and we continued to look for the street address together. Szrulek finished his candy and glanced shyly at me with an occasional half smile; I wished he would say something, anything, but he was silent. I hoped that one day he would get his voice back.

Mama pointed to a building; we had reached our destination at last. We entered a smoky room that held about fifteen to twenty people.

It had been a long time since I had seen so many Jewish men and women in one room who were not afraid of the Nazis. I kept looking and looking, but Papa was not there.

Bits and pieces of conversations surrounded me, filling the room with sadness. They had survived in the sewers, underground bunkers, cellars, attics, concentration camps, and death camps. A few Jewish partisans, who had fought the Germans in the deep forests, were speaking with various people. Some had traveled from distant towns and villages to come here, hoping for a thread of information, for any clue about a mother, father, husband, wife, or child.

Mama wrote our names and the Wojteks' address on a white sheet of paper, which was nailed to what probably was once a white wall and was now smeared with red swastikas and curses wishing death to all the "leftover" Jews. I followed her around the room as she moved from one person to another, repeating the same questions over and over again. "No, no," was always the answer. They did not know anything about Papa, nor about Aunt Elsa, Janek, or my cousins, either.

"No; sorry."

"Niestety."

One man, who had a blond mustache, remembered Papa from before the war, but he said that he had not seen him since 1941. He told Mama that he had survived the war on Aryan papers, posing as a *Volksdeutche* and working for a German firm as a mechanic. He knew he was lucky to have "made it."

A sudden shriek pierced the air, and I saw a darkhaired man with burning black eyes pointing his finger accusingly to the ceiling. "Look, God, what is left of Poland with its millions of Jews! You could squeeze us in the palm of one hand! Are we the last ones left alive, by some mistake?" His shouts drowned out the other voices until two men grabbed him under the arms and briskly tried to lead him outside.

"Where was the world? Why were they silent?" he called out as they pulled him toward the door.

A voice cried out, "I lost my husband and—"

She was interrupted by an angry woman. "I don't want to hear it! I have enough of my own problems!"

She went on to say that she had come from far away, from the Ukraine, to look for her family, who had once lived in Lwów. "I didn't come to hear other people's troubles. I was in Babi Yar, I crawled out from under hundreds of dead bodies. . . . I left my dead baby in that ravine. . . . They kept shooting and we kept falling down . . . just—" She covered her eyes with her hands and started to sob uncontrollably, tears pouring down her pretty face. It was all so terrible, but Mama was already near me, pulling me away to another corner of the room.

"I despise them all, those barbarians!" someone shouted.

"You can't live with hate. It will not help you; it will only destroy you." A frail man looked up at the young woman. "There were some good people too; one of them saved me."

She frowned and pushed her hair from her face. "Oh, yes?" she asked sharply. "Look how many ran to the Gestapo! The Germans could never have done it without the strong support of the locals. You know that!"

"That's for sure," someone agreed. "Did you know that there were more than five death camps in Poland alone?"

Mama told me that it was time for us to go. In a way, I was relieved; everyone was so unhappy. We said good-bye to Szrulek and his father; they were both standing against the wall, surrounded by a small group of people smiling tenderly at the little boy. Then we stepped out into the light and headed toward Bajki Street.

"Maybe tomorrow someone will bring good news for us," she said, not sounding too sure, but trying, as always, to cheer me up.

16

ONE DAY NOT LONG AFTER our trip to the Jewish gathering center, Mama decided to go and see the Christian friends to whom Papa had entrusted our belongings—Grandma Fancia's store merchandise and the suitcases filled with our clothing—in 1939. She told me that she might even bring some clothing back with her right away; I looked forward to seeing it and was disappointed when she returned empty-handed.

She told me that both *Pan* and *Pani* Poznajewski were shocked to see her; they had never expected to lay eyes on her again. *Pan* Poznajewski said that he had only spoken to Papa once during the Nazi occupation. Although, of course, he was very happy to see Mama alive, he and his wife did not know what had happened to the suitcases and boxes filled with our possessions. He was truly sorry, but with all the robberies in these hard times, he was sure she could understand how our things had been stolen. *Pani* Poznajewska added that she too felt bad about it, but "that's how life is." Then they asked about Papa and the rest of our family, wished Mama good luck, and led her to the front door.

Pan Wojtek exploded in fury when Mama told him what had happened. He began to curse the "lying Lucifers" and threatened to "show them," only upsetting Mama even more. She was finally able to calm him down, but she refused to give him their address. When, a few days later, she heard a similar story from the Kołodziez family, who told her that they "did not know" what had happened to her black Persian coat, her silver fox, and our linens, she did not tell *Pan* Wojtek anything about it.

He had been much friendlier to me since the liberation, and Mama told me that she was pleased that we had been getting along well, especially since we would be leaving soon. I could not wait for that day, even though I was not sure where we would be going.

Then one evening, when he thought that I was asleep, *Pan* Wojtek quietly pulled a chair over to our bed and started to whisper to Mama. I pretended that I was sleeping, and with my eyes closed I listened carefully.

After a few coughs, *Pan* Wojtek told Mama that he would like to divorce his wife, marry her, take care of Papa's business and properties—"Let God be with his soul"—and "help the little miss grow up." *Pan* Wojtek continued rapidly, "As you know, my dear *Pani,* it is very dangerous in these unsteady times for a Jewess like you to live alone; it is too much of a risk with all this hatred around, especially after the last, terrible incident." Then he related a story we had already heard from his wife, about the murder of four young boys, survivors of the concentration camps, who had moved together into a little house on the outskirts of Lwów and had been killed in the middle of the night by the local youth.

"I have heard about other killings too. . . . With me, my dear *Pani* Landau, you and the miss would always be safe; no one would ever dare to touch you, God is my witness. I would always take care of you." Here he stopped, cleared his throat, and blew his nose; and as I waited, my face half covered with my blanket, to hear Mama's answer, his wife walked into the room and began to prepare for bed.

I opened my eyes a bit, but all I could distinguish was her shadow silently moving around. I wondered whether she had heard her husband—"the old child," as she called him when he was not acting "like the devil."

Pan Michaj got up, pushed back the chair, and walked to his bed. Mama turned her face toward me; she knew that I was awake and pulled the covers over our heads. "Don't pay any attention to him; we will be moving out soon," she whispered to me. "Let's go to sleep now."

Outside a shrill laugh broke the silence—a drunken soldier? A moment later, a woman's loud scream made us jump up and run to the window, but no one was outside. It was quiet again, but I could not fall asleep. What would happen to us if Papa did not come back? Who would protect us? Mama said that we would be fine, but what made her so sure?

She no longer wanted me to go with her to the meeting place, filled with all those sad and frightening stories. Instead she went alone, still leaning on her cane, still hoping for some news about our family. I stayed

home with *Pani* Krysia, watching the clock and waiting for her return. It was not safe for me to go out
with *Pani* Krysia; many neighbors knew she had
hidden us, and some of them might have been angry
enough to hurt her for keeping Jews. "Who knows
what they might do," she sighed.

I felt lonely on those days, and a nameless fear rested
on my shoulders like an annoying insect that would
not go away. *Pani* Krysia sensed my mood and tried
to lighten it.

We still had a few books that *Pani* Olga had left for
us before she departed for the Carpathian Mountains
to visit a sick cousin. To pass the time I would read
parts of various novels to *Pani* Krysia; she especially
liked the stories of the famous Polish writer Henryk
Sienkiewicz. At other times, we baked cookies, made
fresh marmalade, or rolled the dough for *paluszki* and
pierogi.

I liked being with her and asked her many times if
she would come with us when we moved, but she only
shook her head, smiled, and said that it was too late.
I wished she would change her mind, even though
I knew deep down that she would never leave Staś,
who was now ill with pneumonia. Usually when
Mama came back, *Pani* Krysia was already prepared to
visit her son, and she would depart hastily with her
bags full of food.

Every day, as I waited for Mama, I tried to imagine
that she would surprise me with good news. But she
did not. . . . There was no lead, not even a clue about
Papa. No one knew anything about him, or about the
rest of our family.

As the passing days brought rain and cool breezes,

she continued to inquire. But he was not coming back; I knew it. Some part of me had known for months, but now I understood that it was really so. I remembered something Grandpa Henryk had once said: "If you love someone, he will stay with you forever." And Papa did.

One day Mama came home and told me that she had met a man who had known Papa before the war; he had survived fighting with the Russian partisans. He offered to go with her to the Poznajewski and Kołodzież families to try to get some of our belongings back. This *Pan* Henek was a courageous person, Mama said, and he believed that some of our things might turn up.

A few days later, she went out again and returned home with good news. Our possessions had "suddenly emerged," she said. It seemed that when she had walked into the Poznajewskis' apartment with *Pan* Henek in his partisan uniform covered with Russian medals, this *Pan* and *Pani* had become very nervous. Right away they apologized for being so "forgetful and confused" on Mama's first visit. The wife said that she suddenly remembered where she had hidden the suitcases and boxes.

"We waited in the living room for a while, and then she and her husband brought everything up from the cellar. The same thing happened with the Kołodzież family," Mama said happily.

She wondered aloud if they had been afraid that *Pan* Henek would report them to the Soviet authorities. He was going to bring all our belongings back to the Wojteks' apartment within the next few weeks.

I was curious about this *Pan*. Mama told me that he

had lost a beautiful wife and an eight-month-old baby; after they were killed by Germans, he had escaped to the woods. There he joined the Russian partisans; they all fought the Nazis, though he had experienced a great deal of anti-Semitism among his comrades. They had sent him on the most dangerous sabotage missions and espionage assignments. Mama told me many other interesting stories about him.

I wanted to meet *Pan* Henek, and Mama promised me that he would visit us soon. She explained that he too had been left all alone, but that he still hoped his sister and her family, who lived in Yugoslavia, had somehow survived. Later on he was going to try to find them through the Red Cross. He had an older brother who had left for America just before the war broke out. Of course, *Pan* Henek was sorry he did not go with him, but his life prior to the war had been good—he was a chemical engineer who had owned a pigment factory with his brother and brother-in-law in Czechoslovakia—and he hadn't even thought of leaving Europe until it was too late.

Pan Henek came to visit on a cloudy afternoon that smelled of rain. He was stocky and blond, with an open smile and clear blue eyes, and when he shook my hand, I noticed that his fingers were stained yellow from cigarettes. He sat down opposite me, then carefully placed his tobacco in little pieces of thin paper. Once his handmade cigarettes had been rolled, Mama suggested that the three of us play dominoes.

I asked him many questions, fascinated by his bravery. I liked being with *Pan* Henek, and it wasn't long before we became good friends.

He would come almost daily to visit, and after a

while, he told me he was hoping we could always be together. He wanted to marry Mama, he said, and he would make sure that nothing bad ever happened to me again. I was glad we would not be alone, Mama and I.

A short time later Mama told me that they had found a rooming house on the other side of town, and that after they had signed their marriage document, we were going to leave the Wojteks. And so we did.

At last the day came when we were really moving out. I had thought of this moment for many hours, and now it was here.

Did I only imagine that *Pan* Wojtek's eyes clouded over as he shook hands with me and looked in my eyes for what seemed such a long time? I decided that I did not dislike him any more as he brusquely touched my hair. Then it was time to say good-bye to *Pani* Krysia.

I tried to hold back the tears as she held me in her arms, but then they began to flow and I could not stop them. Who would protect her now? Who would take care of her?

When I whispered in her ear, "Do you want to come with us?" she shook her head and smiled. "I will visit for sure," she said. "Yes, I will. But I can't go."

Pan Henek stood waiting for us in the kitchen as *Pani* Krysia walked with us to the front door. *Pan* Wojtek stayed in the bedroom; I had seen the angry look he gave *Pan* Henek and knew he did not like him. Then we were in the hall, and the door was closing gently.

It was wonderful to be outside, the three of us walking together. Sun flooded the sidewalk and the wind seemed to hold its breath as our footsteps carried us away from the brick building. We turned the corner; Bajki Street was behind us, and ahead lay a new beginning.

Epilogue

WE SLOWLY JOURNEYED toward normalcy again after our move to the rooming house. I took on Henek's last name, and we became a family.

In the room adjoining ours lived a quiet, thin violinist, a Jewish man, who practiced until late into the night—"to catch up on lost time," he said. He remained our friend until we left Lwów.

Henek enrolled me in school, but after a traumatic experience on my first day, when I found a scribbled note in my desk wishing "that Hitler had finished me off," I did not want to return. Mama said I didn't have to go; we would not be staying in the city for long anyway.

Indeed, we didn't stay long in Lwów, even though Henek was offered all kinds of important positions because of his heroic deeds as a partisan. He and Mama were anxious to leave; the N.K.V.D. (the Soviet secret police) was making sudden, unexplained arrests. Night searches that resulted in the confiscation of one's personal belongings were commonplace. No one could be sure what would happen next.

An announcement had been posted, saying that Lwów was going to be annexed to the Soviet Union. As the deadline to leave approached, many people were trying to depart in a hurry. Before long, the streets were flooded with wagons, handcarts, and a few trucks all piled high with furniture, suitcases, and boxes. Others walked or took the tram to the train station.

On our last day, we rode to the station in an old *dorożka*. We passed a red-painted wagon filled with gypsies tightly packed in between bulging boxes. They were the first ones I had seen since the Germans came; they too had been targeted for death. The women looked beautiful with their colorful shawls wrapped around their shoulders; the dark-eyed children were very serious. Behind them, a few gypsy men and young boys followed on foot, carrying large bundles as the noise and excitement of the busy street swirled around them.

The train station was crowded and filled with confusion. The officials checked our papers; everything was in order, and we were granted permission to depart. I was glad we were leaving Lwów behind us forever, with its terrible memories and its bloodstained earth. Our ultimate goal was to find Henek's brother in New York City and eventually emigrate to America, but all of this was a long way off; first we would have to reach Western Europe, the departure point. We would travel through many cities and countries, coming closer to our destination with each stop.

The first one was Przemyśl, now the official border of Poland. There was a tremendous refugee flow from Lwów, and the city was very crowded. After a few hours, we finally were able to get a small room on the third floor of an old building, where we met a few other Jewish people who had survived the war. All were anxious to leave Poland—some for Australia, some for America, and others for Palestine.

We stayed in Przemyśl only a few days and then left for Katowice, where I met Julek, my first new friend. Like me, he had started to collect stamps, and we spent hours exchanging them and playing word games and cards. He had been hidden during the war by his Polish nanny; his parents had survived on Aryan papers. They were hoping to emigrate to Canada, where they had relatives.

Next we headed for Warsaw, where I heard about the heroism of the Jewish people of their ghetto; like Lilliputians defying a monstrous giant, they had risen up to fight the Germans. The uprising had resulted in the deaths of many Germans, but most of the Jews had perished also.

I learned too that in this city the famous Dr. Janusz Korczak, a man of great moral courage, had been offered his freedom by the Nazis if he would abandon the two hundred Jewish orphans who were in his care. He refused to do so; instead, he marched together with them to the train going to the Treblinka death camp and continued to reassure the children almost till the end.

I would hear such stories at night, as Mama and Henek talked to the Jewish neighbors over tea. They too had rejected loneliness and married again, anxious to begin a new life. They would discuss their future plans and hopes or talk about the losses of children, spouses, or parents.

From Warsaw we proceeded to Kraków, where one day, while walking on the main street, Henek stumbled upon an old friend's sixteen-year-old son, an orphan whose parents and entire family had been murdered by the Nazis. Henek brought the boy home, and Siunek became a member of our family and my best friend. We celebrated the end of the war in Kraków in May 1945; the singing and dancing that followed Germany's capitulation spilled out into the streets.

Once the war was over, Henek took Siunek with him to Czechoslovakia. After he found a house in the small town of Teplice, he came back in a little red car to get Mama and me. It was in this town that Uncle Leon from Australia contacted Mama through the Red Cross and asked her to come to Melbourne. He had been informed of the loss of his family and wanted to marry her.

Supposedly my uncle was devastated to learn that Mama already had a husband. Nevertheless, they kept writing to each other, even after he married another woman—a widowed Jewish immigrant from Poland who had been a friend of Aunt Elsa's before the war. Then, months later, Mama asked if he had any photographs of our family; we had none. For some reason, he never answered her again.

In May 1946, in Teplice, my little sister, Bettina, was born, and we had a party in her honor. Shortly thereafter, the Red Cross contacted Henek's brother in New York, and he flew to visit us with his new bride on their honeymoon.

I couldn't wait to meet my first American relatives, my new uncle Bunio and aunt Sylvia. They arrived with trunks full of things and many gifts for all of us.

She was tall and thin with dark hair and a vivid-colored wardrobe that stopped many people in the streets of our small town when we walked together. My English was very poor, and most of the time we just smiled and gestured to each other. Aunt Sylvia had shoes of red, blue, green, black, and yellow; when Mama, who spoke English, translated my question to her—"Do you want to open a shoe store?"—she could not stop laughing.

My aunt was very nice. She dressed me up as a gypsy for a school masquerade party, using lots of American make-up; when I won my first prize, she was delighted.

Uncle Bunio, older than his wife, was short and heavyset with friendly, smiling eyes and lots of little wrinkles below them. He was anxious to show Aunt Sylvia both the surrounding countryside, which he knew from when he lived here with Henek before the war, and Prague with its museums and antiques stores. Antiques were his business in New York.

Since my uncle still spoke Polish, we were able to understand each other, and I listened with fascination to his descriptions of New York with its skyscrapers. I was anxious to see it all for myself, as soon as he could get us our visas.

My aunt and uncle stayed for a few weeks, visiting many places of interest including the Pinkas synagogue, inscribed with the names of over 77,000 people who had been murdered by the Nazis; and Terezin, the ghetto-camp where thousands of innocent Jewish men, women, and children had been murdered. Aunt Sylvia said she could not take it; she was getting too upset, and she didn't want to tour "such sad places." But my uncle did not think the same way; he told his brother that he was eager to see everything, now that he was here, and Henek agreed that this was important.

We had a lovely villa in Czechoslovakia, and our life was comfortable there. I went to school, started to learn Czech, made a couple of friends, and had my first pet—a beautiful parrot that was a surprise gift from Henek. Lora became my constant companion; she wouldn't fly away even when I walked outside with her on my shoulder. She would perch there and talk to me.

My mother and Henek also made new friends, and played chess; Mama played the piano again, and our house vibrated with the melodies of her favorite composers. It was from here that Mama sent the first of many packages to the Wojteks.

Before we left for Paris, an aunt of Siunek's from Australia found out through the Red Cross that he was alive and came to take him back with her. They later emigrated to Israel, which finally became the Jewish homeland; he stayed in touch and we still correspond to this day.

We went by train to Paris in 1948 and remained there for a few months. It was a very exciting city, with lots of wonderful art to see; I was nearly overcome by my first trip to the Louvre. Mama started to teach me French, and after a while I knew enough to go grocery shopping near the small hotel-apartment where we stayed.

Henek was able to locate his sister, who had escaped from a labor camp in Yugoslavia together with her husband and their two children, Rózia and Józek; they had joined the partisans in the woods. The camp had been guarded by Italian Fascists, who were not as cruel and merciless as the Eastern European ones.

Henek kept in touch with his sister, and eventually he took a train to visit her in Yugoslavia. Like us, her family was hoping to emigrate as soon as possible, leaving the European tragedy behind them.

He was also happy to discover his cousin Renia, a pianist, was alive, and he traveled to see her as well. She had survived with her mother by hiding for two years in a bunker on the outskirts of a Polish village with the help of a peasant and a forester. Their underground hiding place, covered by branches and leaves, was on a heavily wooded mountaintop, which discouraged shepherds from climbing there with their flocks. After being liberated by the Red Army, Renia was protected from the peasants by the Russian officers for whom she played the piano. She and her mother at last were allowed to leave Poland to be reunited with her brother in Sweden.

After Henek returned from seeing Renia in Stockholm, he told me a story that he'd heard from a Hungarian who was saved by a Swedish diplomat, Raoul Wallenberg. This story left a lasting impact on me. Concerned with the injustice perpetrated on the Jews, Wallenberg had decided to do something about it. Using the protection of his neutral country, he had traveled to Budapest, set up a special mission there, and began to print Swedish passports for Hungarian Jews, including many children whose parents were killed. By personally handing out these passports, in many instances even getting people off the death train to Auschwitz, he saved thousands of lives.

In Paris I met Henek's sister's son, Józek, who had left Yugoslavia to study dentistry. He took me to my first grown-up dance at the University; I was only thirteen and was probably the youngest person there. I still remember how proudly I wore my new black-and-white rabbit coat, and how I worried, while dancing and having a wonderful time, that someone would steal it from the cloakroom.

From Paris we proceeded to Amsterdam, where we remained until our visas arrived. Nowhere else had I ever felt as comfortable as I did in Holland; it became my adopted country as I went to school, learned the language, and made new friends.

The charming city, with its picturesque *grachten* (canals), colorful flowers, friendly people, and many museums was at last a place where I no longer felt discriminated against. I was free to be just who and what I was—a teenager interested in boys, friends, and art. We spent many days sightseeing, but my favorite place was the Rijksmuseum with its magnificent works of Rembrandt, Vermeer, Van Eyck, Breughel, and many other Masters. I still keep in touch with my friends from this time.

After I emigrated to the United States in December 1951, I married, raised two children, and continued my education, of which art was an integral part. In 1990 I visited Amsterdam with my husband and my mother; many things had changed, but the city still holds enchanted memories for me.

My children are married now with babies of their own. Danielle, Stefan, Sasha, Alexei, and Joshua bring us tremendous joy, and I hope that the rains in their lives will never be too severe.

Dr. Nelly S. Toll came to America in 1951. She holds a master's degree in art and art history and education from Rutgers University, has studied at the Academy of Fine Arts in Philadelphia, and received her Ph.D. from the University of Pennsylvania. She has exhibited her adult work widely and has taught both art and art history. Dr. Toll also holds a master's degree in counseling from Glassboro College and a degree in art therapy from Hahnemann University; she has combined both fields as a counselor working with young people.

Her sixty-four watercolor paintings from the thirteen months she spent in hiding in Poland during World War II have been shown around the world. Eight are in the permanent collection of the Yad Vashem Museum in Israel.

She is also the co-author of a play based on her wartime experiences and the author of *Without Surrender: Art of the Holocaust,* a subject on which she lectures frequently. She presently teaches Humanities at Drexel University and the University of Pennsylvania.